The Missouri Harmony

THE MISSOURI HARMONY

Or a Collection of
Psalm and Hymn Tunes, and Anthems

An Introduction to the Grounds and Rudiments of Music

BY ALLEN D. CARDEN

*To Which Is Added
A Supplement*

Introduction to the Bison Book Edition
by Shirley Bean

University of Nebraska Press
Lincoln and London

Introduction to the Bison Book Edition © 1994 by the
University of Nebraska Press

First Bison Book printing: 1994
Most recent printing indicated by the last digit below:
10   9   8   7   6   5   4   3   2   1

Library of Congress Cataloging-in-Publication Data
The Missouri harmony, or, A collection of psalm and hymn tunes, and anthems: an introduction to the grounds and rudiments of music / (compiled)
by Allen D. Carden; to which is added a supplement; introduction to the Bison book edition by Shirley Bean.
p.   cm.
Originally published: 9th ed. Cincinnati: Phillips and Reynolds, 1846.
ISBN 0-8032-6114-4 (pa)
1. Choruses, Sacred (Mixed voices), Unaccompanied.   2. Tune-books.   3.
Hymns, English.   4. Shape note hymnals.   I. Carden, Allen D., 1792–
1859.   II. Title: Missouri harmony.   III. Title: Collection of psalm and
hymn tunes, and anthems.
M2117.M67   1994
93-41235   CIP
M

This Bison Book edition duplicates the 1846 reprint of the ninth edition,
published by Phillips and Reynolds, Cincinnati. The Supplement was added
to the seventh edition in 1835.

∞

ACKNOWLEDGMENTS

This facsimile edition was made possible through the generosity of Mr. Raymond C. Hamrick of Macon, Georgia, who made his original edition available for the project. Thanks also go to the St. Louis Shape Note Singers for their interest and support.

·

The ninth edition (1840) was chosen for this Bison Book reprint because it appears to have been one of the most widely used editions of *The Missouri Harmony*. Its popularity was reflected by reprintings in 1841, 1842, 1844, 1846 (this facsimile), and 1848.

INTRODUCTION

By Shirley Bean

The Missouri Harmony was the quintessential frontier tune book. This compilation of popular hymn tunes in shape-note notation had a thirty-eight-year publishing history which greatly exceeded that of other tune books of the period. The tune book's longevity was due in part to its wide use by singing school masters during the nineteenth century in teaching people to read music. It contained the largest collection of what was termed the "old melodies," more suited for solemn worship, as well as more modern compositions of the time, making it one of the best tune books for the use of congregations or choirs. Its uniqueness stems from the fact that it was originally compiled to appeal to the stylistic tastes of southern rural singers but was later "urbanized" by the publisher. Thus, an already popular collection was transformed into one that would gain the acceptance of those who preferred the northern urban style of hymn setting, a style which grew in popularity during the mid to late nineteenth century.

Tune books and singing schools played an important role in teaching music to frontier Americans. The tune books contained theoretical information and instruction in singing in their introductions and continued the American tradition of using shaped notes as an aid to students who were learning to read music. An obvious advantage of shape-note notation was that it made all keys one. For singers who had learned the shapes, keys were unnecessary; it was thought easier to learn notes represented by shapes than through positions on a staff.[1]

The desire of settlers to participate in the congregational singing in their churches provided the necessary motivation for learning to sing by note. On the frontier this goal was achieved through the development of shape-notation and its dissemination by tune-compilers and singing masters.

The songs used in teaching music were mostly sacred in nature. But the environment in which they were taught became, in time, delightfully secular, thereby diminishing the preponderant influence of the churches.

Singing schools were not formal institutions, as their name would seem to suggest. They were simply a four- to six-week term of instruction in vocal music, held one or two nights per week. Extravagant claims for their effectiveness were not made, but the churchgoers enrolled could look forward to singing, to learning something useful, and to socializing.

In urban areas, singing schools were often sponsored by the local churches. They took the responsibility of securing a teacher and providing a neutral meeting place such as the town courthouse or even a local tavern.

Those held in the tavern furnished fuel for pious conservatives who felt that the singing master's talents were frequently a gift from the spirit (not necessarily Divine in nature) and that too much socializing took place during intermission and after the lesson. The tavern-keeper, however, made the rental cheap in consideration of the patronage that his barroom enjoyed during recess and afterward.

The singing masters who taught singing schools were itinerants whose lives were spent traveling the countryside, setting up and teaching schools, only to move on when the term was over.[2] Among them was the occasional minister who was more highly educated than his colleagues. To attract favorable attention to themselves and to their schools, as well as to gain increased remuneration, some compiled, published, and sold their own tune books, often giving them regional titles.[3]

COMPILATION AND PUBLICATION

It was from this tradition that *The Missouri Harmony* emerged. Singing-master Allen Carden first introduced the collection for use in his St. Louis singing school in 1820. It was the first tune book from the Missouri Territory (which would become a state in 1821). Carden did not compose any tunes for his book but merely compiled popular ones from tune books already in use. He relied heavily upon Ananias Davisson's *Kentucky Harmony* (1816), as 111 of the 185 tunes appear to have been taken from Davisson. Carden also borrowed tunes from John Wyeth's *Repository of Sacred Music. Part Second* (1813), Freeman Lewis's *The Beauties of Harmony* (1814), and Nathan Chapin and Joseph Dickerson's *The Musical Instructor* (1808).

In selecting tunes from a standard repertory of established favorites, Carden demonstrated a sure sense of what would please the prospective purchaser. What he did not anticipate, however, was that *The Missouri Harmony* would become a preeminent tune book of the day and would enjoy great success, going through ten editions and numerous reprintings from 1820 through the late 1850s.

One of these copies evidently fell into the hands of young Abraham Lincoln, for it was said by settlers of the time that Lincoln and his sweetheart, Ann Rutledge, sang from *The Missouri Harmony* in the Rutledge tavern in New Salem.[4] Ultimately, other tune book compilers throughout the country began using Carden's book as a resource, as demonstrated in the North (*Juvenile Harmony*), South (*Southern Harmony*), and West (*St. Louis Harmony*).

Initially, Carden encountered a major obstacle in attempting to compile his tune book. At that time, St. Louis did not possess a font of type for setting shaped-notation, and thus Carden was forced to have the book printed where such type was readily available. It was only natural that he work with a printer in Cincinnati, since Cincinnati was becoming the most western center for the manufacture of printing presses, equipment, and the casting of type. Prior to 1820, the fonts of musical type available in Cincinnati had undoubtedly been purchased and shipped from the East—a very expensive procedure. Thereafter, Cincinnati quickly became the center of shaped-note publishing, and far more tune book collections were brought out in Cincinnati that in any other town, or even region, in the country. Charles Hamm suggested that if the city had not already been blessed with a surplus of nicknames during the first half of the nineteenth century, it might well have been dubbed the "Patent Note Mecca."[5]

Carden succeeded in establishing a working relationship with publisher Ephraim Morgan and the printing firm of Morgan, Lodge, & Co. The Morgan firm was integral to the far-reaching success of *The Missouri Harmony* through its many editions and reprintings. Undoubtedly, the success of *The Missouri Harmony* contributed in turn to the success of the Morgan firm.

The Missouri Harmony is representative in style, content, and format of the sixteen frontier tune books that preceded it. It was printed in oblong form; some of the earlier copies were bound in boards with leather backs or in full leather. The book contains the traditional theoretical introduction, followed by 173 tunes (in the style of hymn tunes or fuguing pieces) and 12 anthems.[6] Many of the tunes are based on melodies or melodic fragments that were a part of the Celtic background of early American settlers. The tunes possess the same discernible affinity for unique arrangements of diatonic scales and modality that is found in the English ballads and love songs which had been popular in the British Isles for over two centuries.

Although the texts are most often doctrinal or moralistic, the tunes are frequently derived from *contrafactum*, the common prac-

tice of putting new words to old songs or folk tunes. An obvious example is found in the tune "Captain Kidd" (p. 57). The title of the ballad that describes the hanging of Captain Kidd in 1701 is retained, but the ballad itself has been replaced by a sacred text. Other examples include "New Orleans" (p. 28), from the secular ballad "Greenwood Siding," and the traditional ballad "Lord Thomas and Fair Elenor."

Carden included thirty-seven fuguing tunes in his compilation. "Lenox" (p. 23) by Lewis Edson (1746–1820) is a typical example as are the tunes "Sherburne" (p. 98) and "Russia" (p. 53) by Daniel Read (1757–1836). Ten additional tunes utilize imitation to a lesser degree and many of the anthems also make use of fuguing sections. William Billings (1746–1800) is represented by the set piece "David's Lamentation" (p. 162), by his "Easter Anthem" (p. 163), his "Funeral Anthem" (p. 174), and by the anthem "The Rose of Sharon" (p. 175).

Carden purchased a font of music type in 1824 in Nashville, and it would seem that he intended to take over the printing of *The Missouri Harmony* himself. From all indications, however, he had nothing more to do with the book after its use in St. Louis. All later editions were published by Cincinnati publishers and Carden had no editorial role or financial interest in the book after 1824. The only mention of *The Missouri Harmony* in St. Louis at a later date is found in an 1831 advertisement in the *St. Louis Times* announcing *"KIRKHAM'S GRAMMAR & MISSOURI HARMONY,* just received and for sale, at the Drug and Book store, corner of Main and Market Streets."[7] The book became commercial property (much like *The Worcester Collection, Village Harmony,* and *The Easy Instruc-*

Table 1

Publishing Lineage of *The Missouri Harmony*

Edition	Issue	Publisher(s)	Printer(s)	Special Features	Stereotyper
[First]	1820	The Compiler (Carden, St. Louis)	Morgan, Lodge, & Co. (Cincinnati)		
[Second]	1825	Morgan, Lodge, & Fisher	Morgan, Lodge, & Fisher		
[Third]	1827	Drake & Conclin	Morgan, Fisher, & L'Hommedieu		
[Fourth]	1829	Morgan & Sanxay	Morgan & Sanxay	First stereotyped edition	Oliver Wells & Co.
[Fifth]	1830	Morgan & Sanxay	Morgan & Sanxay		Oliver Wells & Co.
	1831	Morgan & Sanxay	Morgan & Sanxay	Copyrighted	
[Sixth]	1832	Morgan & Sanxay	Morgan & Sanxay	Revised & improved	Oliver Wells & Co.
	1833	Morgan & Sanxay	Morgan & Sanxay		
	1834	Morgan & Sanxay	Morgan & Sanxay		
[Seventh]	1835	Morgan & Sanxay	Morgan & Sanxay	Supplement added	Not indicated but Wells continued as stereotyper until 1850
	1836	Morgan & Sanxay	Morgan & Sanxay		
	1837	E. Morgan & Son	E. Morgan & Son		
[Eighth]	1838	E. Morgan & Son	E. Morgan & Son		
	1839	E. Morgan & Co.	E. Morgan & Co.		
[Ninth]	1840	E. Morgan & Co.	E. Morgan & Co.	Latest improved edition	
	1841	E. Morgan & Co.	E. Morgan & Co.		
	1842	E. Morgan & Co.	E. Morgan & Co.		
	1844	Phillips & Reynolds	Phillips & Reynolds		
	1846	Phillips & Reynolds	Phillips & Reynolds		
	1848	Phillips & Reynolds	Phillips & Reynolds		
[Tenth]	1850	Wm. Phillips & Co.	Not indicated for this edition	Revised, enlarged corrected	E. Morgan & Co. (continued through 1858)
	1854?	Moore, Wilstach, & Keys			
	1855	Moore, Wilstach, Keys, & Overend			
	1857	Moore, Wilstach, Keys, & Overend			
	1858?	Moore, Wilstach, Keys, & Co.			

tor), administered and exploited by businessmen, not musicians.

By 1825, the Morgan firm recognized the inherent usefulness of Carden's collection of tunes and published a second edition, followed by a third edition in 1827 (Table 1).[8] Morgan made no changes in the contents and advertised the book as "a highly approved Music Book." At that time the tune book sold for a dollar per copy and nine dollars per dozen.

Sales were probably relatively low until the late 1820s, when demand for the tune book increased enough to justify a stereotyped edition in 1829. The object of stereotyping was to permit small issues of publications at a time. This limited large surplus should the book not prove salable and facilitated reprints should there be sufficient demand for repeated issues.[9] Morgan's decision to stereotype *The Missouri Harmony* was significant, as it tended to freeze Carden's compilation for later editions.

ADDITION OF THE SUPPLEMENT

Because of the tune book's increasing popularity, Morgan's firm continued to produce new editions and issues without making any major alterations, even though the designation "Revised and Improved" would be used. A substantial change occurred, however, with the seventh edition in 1835. A Supplement "BY AN AMATEUR" was added that contained twenty-three hymn tunes, four choral numbers, a sacred song, and a duet. Unlike the portion that Carden compiled, the Supplement establishes the identity of many of the composers and identifies Isaac Watts as the author of the majority of the texts. The most striking feature of the Supplement is that it would have appealed to those who preferred the emerging "genteel" style, in direct contrast to the rest of the tune book, which remains unchanged from previous editions.[10]

Speculation about the identity of the compiler of the Supplement necessarily begins with the designation "Amateur." According to the usage of the day, such a description simply indicated that the individual so named was not a professional musician, but a well-rounded and educated gentleman.[11] The Supplement was obviously a welcome addition, as it appeared in all subsequent editions and issues of the tune book.

In 1840, the ninth edition was published as the "Latest Improved Edition." It appears to have been one of the most popular editions, as reflected by its reissuance in 1841, 1842, 1844, 1846 (the reprinting duplicated here), and 1848, with the last three issues "Printed and Published by Phillips and Reynolds." There is no evidence to indicate that Morgan's firm ever published *The Missouri Harmony* after 1841, but the firm did succeed Oliver Wells and Company as stereotyper of the 1850 edition.[12] Publication was taken over by Phillips and Reynolds and their successors. Both William Phillips and Sackett Reynolds had been employees in Morgan's firm prior to opening their own publishing firm in 1844. This ninth edition is undoubtedly the one offered for sale (for fifty cents) by Morgan's firm in a lengthy advertisement appearing in *Shaffer's Advertising Directory*.[13]

WARREN'S EDITION

The transition of Cincinnati from a small town to metropolitan status in the middle of the nineteenth century resulted from a temporary combination of four influences. These included an indigenous musical tradition, a thriving music publishing business, the genius of half a dozen local composers, and the growing abundance of private music teachers.

Concerts, sacred and secular, had become very fashionable. The minstrel shows of Dan Emmett from Mt. Vernon, Ohio, and Stephen Foster, one-time resident of Cincinnati, were delighting people. There was a broadening of the basis of musical life achieved through more widespread private music instruction, the improvement of steamboat travel (with its advantages in bringing musicians from New Orleans and eastern states), new concert halls, and the increase in numbers of professional musicians. Grandiose prize concerts were in vogue during the 1850s. The best musicians of the city performed; a promoter managed the affair, and crowds were lured not so much by the artistry of the musicians, as by the imposing list of prizes.[14]

Music was introduced into the Cincinnati school system in 1845 with William F. Coburn as the first teacher. Charles Aiken, who, next to Lowell Mason, was considered one of the pioneers of public school music, succeeded Coburn in 1848. He compiled the *Cincinnati Music Readers* for the elementary schools, the *High School Choralist* and the *Choralist's Companion*. In 1857, Cincinnati brought Luther Whiting Mason in to introduce music in the primary grades. The emphasis on music in the schools was accompanied by the founding of numerous institutions for broader musical training.[15]

The abundant singing societies and choral organizations also had considerable influence in the musical education of the period. These societies before 1848 were made up mostly of English, German, Welsh, and Swiss singers who participated primarily for their own enjoyment and the pleasure of the public. In 1848, a group of German choral organizations in the vicinity of Cincinnati jointly presented a program of German folk songs and choral music. As a consequence, a union was formed among the organizations from Cincinnati, Louisville, and Madison (Indiana), resulting in the holding of a *Saengerfest* in June 1849.[16] By 1857, the well-trained chorus of the Welsh Church was upholding the musical reputation of Cincinnati with an *Eisteddfod* festival.

Over sixty musicians, music teachers, and "Professors of Music" are listed in *Williams' Cincinnati Directory and Business Advertiser*. Charles Warren, one of the "professors," was chosen by the publisher to transform the harmonizations of *The Missouri Harmony* to reflect the emerging urban style in Cincinnati. This tenth edition was published by Wm. Phillips and Company and stereotyped by E. Morgan and Company in 1850. It was reissued in 1855 and 1857 by the publisher Moore, Wilstach, Keys and Overend. There may also have been issues in 1854 and 1858.

Ernst C. Krohn mentions that the label on the front cover of the 1857 issue is identical with the title page for the 1850 issue, with the exception of "Moore, Wilstach, and Keys, Publishers," and is dated 1854. The date could indicate the existence of an 1854 issue. However, Krohn further states that the fact the label has an ornamental border would prove that it is not an actual 1854 title page.[17] All earlier labels are reproductions of the current title pages, but without dates. This label and the one for the possible 1858 issue are the only extant dated covers. A reproduction of the title page, however, was frequently glued to both covers of the tune book. At times, an older title page was used so that the label did not always agree with the actual title page. A label on the cover of a copy of the 1857 issue is dated 1858. Until actual copies of the 1854 and 1858 issues are discovered, their publication must remain in doubt. The dated labels alone are not conclusive.

The Preface to Warren's edition attests to the merits and continued popularity of the tune book and indicates that the initiative for this "new edition" came from the publishers:

> In presenting this New Edition of the Missouri Harmony to the public, the publishers take the privilege of saying a few words in its favor. It has been long known to possess the merit of having the largest collection of what may be termed the old melodies, and which are identified with our most hallowed emotions, and which are undoubtedly more suited to solemn worship than perhaps any other selection. It also abounds with the most beautiful of the more modern compositions, making it altogether one of the best works for the use of Congregations or Choirs now in use.

The Preface further informs us of the reason for this reworked edition. Earlier printings had "several errors in the harmony." But the work was highly regarded because it contained "more of the primitive tunes than any other work of the same size." This caused the "publishers to have it revised and corrected" by the "scientific musician" (meaning professionally trained) Charles Warren.

The format of the introductory sections remains essentially the same as in the earlier editions. The original text, diagrams, and musical examples are identical in content but, at times, are rearranged on the page. The titles to Parts I, II, and III remain the same, with the Supplement now incorporated as Part IV. The title of the Supplement is maintained but there is no reference to it being a Supplement; also, the line "BY AN AMATEUR" is omitted.

Warren abandoned the use of the alto (C clef), which was used in the former editions, and used the G clef "for the reason that the G clef is more generally known and practiced in works of this kind, and the same part can also be sung by a second treble voice." Since the alto part in the Supplement was placed on the upper staff, which was inconsistent with the rest of the tune book, Warren renamed the staves. The top staff is now called the tenor voice, the second staff is for the alto part, the third staff for the treble, and the lower staff for the bass voice.

In earlier editions the first tune began on page twenty-one, as there was a continuum of numerals from beginning to end. But in 1850, after twenty pages of theory, the first page containing the tune "Primrose" was renumbered "one," thus starting a new series of pagination for the tunes.

All tunes retained their two-, three-, and four-part settings. In numerous tunes the meter signature was changed from duple to triple to allow strong textual and metric accents to coincide. Others maintained the same meter signature but changed the bar-lines that are shifted in earlier editions by the lengthening of a note at the end of a phrase or by introducing a rest at the beginning of a phrase.

The tunes themselves remained basically intact. The biggest break with earlier editions was in the harmonizations (Figures 1 and 2). The "errors" found in the earlier editions were corrected. Parallelisms, unprepared and unresolved dissonances, incomplete chords, and retrogressive patterns were corrected. The settings were

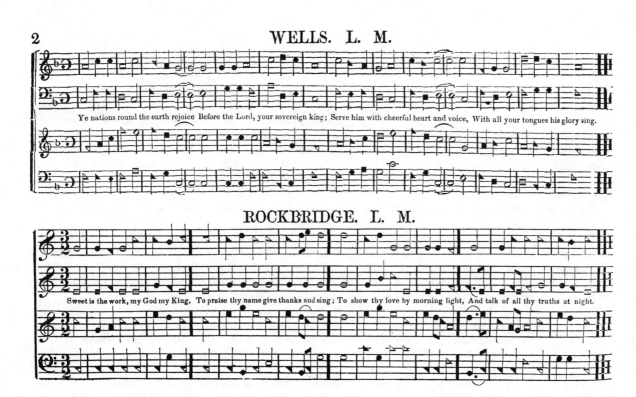

Fig. 1. Rockbridge (1846 edition), 22.
Fig. 2. Rockbridge (1850 edition), 2.

conceived harmonically rather than contrapuntally. There is a lack of rhythmic independence of each part, extensive use of repeated pitches in the accompanying parts, and many bass parts become very static. By contrast, in the earlier editions some of the accompanying parts rivaled the tune for melodiousness.

By the time of Warren's edition, the four-shape tune books no longer had a stranglehold on the market. There was a flurry of tune book activity of seven-shapes in Cincinnati and most of the collections printed with seven-shapes promoted the new reform of church music led by such men as Thomas Hastings, Solomon Warriner, and the Mason brothers, which had engulfed most of the East and was now sweeping into the western country. The publisher, in having this edition "revised and corrected," was undoubtedly attempting to bring one of the most popular and approved tune books into line with the "correct" scientific taste that was the language of the Masons and progressive improvement.

ALLEN D. CARDEN, COMPILER

According to the dates inscribed on his tombstone, Allen Dickenson Carden was born October 13, 1792, and died October 18, 1859. Family Bible records indicate that the Carden family migrated from Fincastle, Botetourt County, Virginia, to Williamsport, Maury County, Tennessee.[18] From there the family moved to Franklin (about forty miles south of Nashville) in Williamson County, Tennessee. In the concluding remarks on the last page of the *Kentucky Harmony,* Davisson offers his thanks to the "gentlemen teachers in Virginia, Tennessee, and Kentucky" who were helpful to him. Carden's name is included in the list, along with the names of eleven other teachers.

In the May 31, 1820, issue of the *Missouri Gazette,* published in St. Louis, Thomas Essex advertised "Vocal Music Books, *The Missouri Harmony,* just published and for sale." This may have been the first public announcement of Carden's book of psalm and hymn tunes. In this same issue, Carden publicized "a School for teaching the theory and practice of Vocal Music" and stated:

> Gentlemen and Ladies of this town, who wish to acquire a knowledge of this art, are hereby respectfully informed that an opportunity is now presented them. The school will commence on Tuesday, the 30th inst., at 3 o'clock P.M. and by candle light the same evening in the Baptist church, and continue every Tuesday and Friday.

The fate of Carden's singing school is not known. Since these classes usually lasted from four to six weeks, Carden was probably in St. Louis at least through June 1820. He was not listed in the first City Directory of St. Louis issued in 1821. It is likely that he had already moved on to Nashville, Tennessee.

The family Bible indicates that Carden married Maria W. Hyde on December 4, 1823, and that she had been born July 22, 1807, in Tennessee. It also lists four children (three girls and one boy) born to the Cardens.

In 1824, with the assistance of Samuel J. Rogers, F. Moore and J. Green, Carden published at Nashville *The Western Harmony,* and in 1829, *The United States Harmony*. The following advertisement was placed by Carden in the *Nashville Republican* on April 10, 1824:

> Now in the press, at the Nashville Republican office, and will be published with all possible speed, *The Western Harmony, A New and Im-*

proved Music Book. To contain 150 pages, selected and published for the use of the Methodist, Baptist, Presbyterian, and all other Christian churches in the Western country. The editor of this book has purchased music type, for the purpose of keeping up an uniform system of music—that there may be a little more harmony in the music of the different churches. Teachers are invited to call or send for a copy and examine for themselves.—The book will be sold as low as any other ever published. All letters or orders directed to the editor will be punctually attended to. Nashville, April 10.   A.D. Carden, Editor

We presume that Carden continued to be active in the musical life of Nashville since an advertisement for his third tune book, *The United States Harmony,* appeared in the *National Banner and Nashville Whig* on September 29, 1829. The 1830 and 1840 Census show that he was still in Nashville. Furthermore, deed records indicate Carden acquired land in the Nashville area (Davidson County) in 1834, 1837, and 1839.[19]

As early as 1835, tax records indicate Carden was taxed for one white poll and two black polls, but no land, in Maury County, Tennessee.[20] Tax records for 1836 and 1837 indicate a residence in Williamsport (Maury County), two slaves, one carriage, and one white poll.

Records reveal he was also involved in property transactions in Stewart County, Tennessee, in 1837 and 1839 (over four thousand acres) and in Carroll County in 1847 and 1849.[21] the Williamson County tax records for 1848 indicate Carden had two slaves, two lots, one carriage, and one piano (valued at two hundred dollars).

He was a member of the Freemasons and belonged to Hiram Lodge No. 7 in Franklin, Tennessee, which still uses the same building constructed in 1823.[22] Maria Carden died June 3, 1858, followed by Carden on October 18, 1859. Both were buried in the Rest Haven Cemetery in Franklin, Tennessee.

Carden's career was entirely typical of the singing master and tune book compiler. He pursued music through his youth, achieved some wealth and experience, then settled down to other activities.

EPHRAIM MORGAN, PUBLISHER

Ephraim Morgan was a typical Cincinnatian of the first generation in that he was a native easterner, born in Brimfield, Massachusetts, in 1790. He began his long career in Cincinnati in 1805 as a printer's devil in *The Western Spy* office, where he beat many forms with inky buckskin balls with no way of imagining a future in which his own printing plant, the largest in the city, would contain automatically inked power presses.[23] By 1826, he was the senior partner in the firm of Morgan, Lodge, Fisher, and L'Hommedieu when that company established the *Cincinnati Daily Gazette,* which had the distinction of being the first daily paper published west of the Allegheny Mountains.[24] The printing firm became involved in tune book publishing with the 1825 edition of *The Missouri Harmony* and the 1829 edition of W. C. Knight's *Juvenile Harmony.*

In 1828, Morgan withdrew from this company because of his opposition to the paper's policy of running advertisements for the return of fugitive slaves. He established a separate book printing and publishing business with John Sanxay as his associate for several years. The house of Morgan and Sanxay published many books, the majority of which were standard religious and educational works, including *The Missouri Harmony*.[25]

While continuing his publishing activities, Morgan also built, in partnership with his sons, the largest printing office in the West, including stereotyping and binding departments. In 1829, Morgan and Sanxay issued the first stereotyped edition of *The Missouri Harmony*. Morgan's power presses accounted for a good share of Cincinnati's importance as a publishing center. Numerous advertisements by Morgan's firm indicate that, by 1841, he had "five power presses propelled by water, each of which could throw off 5,000 impressions daily."[26] Morgan continued publishing, in partnership with his sons, until his death in 1873.

CHARLES WARREN, PROFESSOR

Charles Warren was responsible for the "corrected" edition of *The Missouri Harmony,* published in 1850. He is listed in John W. Moore's *Dictionary of Musical Information* as "a noted teacher of music in Ohio, published, 1850, an edition of "the Missouri Harmony," with modern harmony; 270 pages."[27]

Very little information about Warren has survived. He and his wife, Elizabeth, were both born in England; he in January 1809, and she in 1820.[28] The Warrens had one daughter who was born in New York. The 1850 Census for Cincinnati listed the daughter as age thirteen, indicating that the Warrens had arrived in this country by the year 1837.

When he moved his family to Cincinnati late in the year 1848 or early in 1849, Warren was in his early forties. At the time of his arrival, Cincinnati was a thriving city whose population had grown to 115,438, representing an increase of 150 percent since 1840.[29] It was at this time he was approached by Wm. Phillips and Company to edit and modernize *The Missouri Harmony*.

Warren was first listed as a "teacher of music" in the City Directory for 1849–1850. His address at this time was on the "north side of 5th between Mill and Stone."[30] Warren resided there until 1875, when he moved to 73 Kemper Street in Walnut Hills, a fashionable residential section that forty years earlier had included the home of Harriet Beecher Stowe.

After 1875, the only known information regarding Warren is found in the annual City Directory of Cincinnati, in which his name continued to appear until his death in 1884. The *Enquirer* published the following notice of his death:

> WARREN—At his late residence, Kemper street, near Park avenue, Walnut Hills, at 2 P.M., November 24th, Professor Charles Warren, aged 76 years and 10 months. Funeral Wednesday, November 26th, at 11 o'clock A.M. Burial private. No flowers.[31]

Warren's wife continued to be listed (as his widow) in the annual directories until her death in 1897.

Warren was a foreign-born professional recruited by the publishers to make a silk purse out of what must have been increasingly regarded as a sow's ear. Among the best indicators of musical change is that the publishers, who in 1835 had employed an "amateur" to improve the book, now sought a "professor."

NOTES TO INTRODUCTION

1. The shapes have inherent charm and interest in themselves. Fa (or faw) is represented by $\triangle$, sol by $\bigcirc$, la (or law) by $\square$, and mi by $\diamondsuit$. The shapes could be read by anyone trained in conventional (round-note) notation and even when words were being sung, the shapes were continually before the singer as a constant reminder of the syllables and degrees of the sale. The reverse, unfortunately, was not true. Those who initially learned to read using shapes, could not read round-note notation. The shape-noters met with strong resistance from the round-note conservatives who called the shape-note symbols "buckwheat grains" and the music they represented "three-cornered sounds," "measle-toed music," or "shirt-sleeves music" fit only for the ignorant and uncultured. The shape-note liberals retaliated with equally derisive terms, calling the round-noters "roundheads" and their music "coat and tails music," "monkish music," or "music for snobs."

2. The singing master often appeared with a blackboard, charts showing tonal steps and their changes with keys, a pointer, pitchpipe, an armful of tune books, a love for music, and an earnest desire to teach people to sing. The hopeful scholars brought firewood, slates or lapboards, candles, and an eagerness to learn the art of singing. The candles were sealed to the corners of the slates or boards to supply light. Seating was usually arranged in a semicircle several rows deep. Instruction commenced with a presentation of the rudiments of music, emphasizing shaped notation (or conventional notation, if the singing master was of the round note persuasion), the gamut, staves, "cliffs," keys, note lengths, and moods of time. Soon the group was given exercises in voice placement called "lessons for tuning the voice," (pp. 17–19). Finally, the class was divided into four groups, each singer assigned an appropriate part, and part-singing of familiar songs was undertaken. Songs were first sung by syllables, each part at a time with many repetitions. Words were not allowed until each part had been thoroughly mastered. All were taught to beat time in the various "moods" as they sang. After achieving some proficiency in sight-singing and part-singing, the class concentrated on the main goal—mastery of new songs.

3. Double vocations were not unusual. If the area proved to be profitable, the singing master set up a more permanent residency and frequently became involved in local politics, farming, or some other trade. Supply Belcher (1751–1836), compiler of *The Harmony of Maine* in 1794, was a school teacher, tavern-keeper, and local politician. Singing master Justin Morgan (1747–1798), who compiled no tune book of his own but contributed to many, including *The Missouri Harmony,* bred horses and was a town clerk. William Billings (1746–1800), one of the most prolific singing masters, was a tanner by trade. Daniel Read (1757–1836), composer, compiler, and publisher of sacred music, was also a manufacturer of ivory combs.

4. W. H. Venable, *Beginnings of Literary Culture in the Ohio Valley: Historical and Biographical Sketches* (Cincinnati: Robert Clarke and Company, 1891), 195.

5. Charles Hamm, "Patent Notes in Cincinnati," *Ohio Historical and Philosophical Society Bulletin,* XVI (October 1958); 293–310. Fifteen tune books (including *The Missouri Harmony*) were published between 1813 and 1836. Shape-noters frequently called their symbols "patent notes" with reference to a patent having been obtained for the invention. In 1798, William Little had obtained a copyright for *The Easy Instructor,* which did not appear in print until 1801. On May 12, 1802, the United States government granted Andrew Law a patent on his system of notation.

6. The fuguing (fuging) tune is basically a hymn tune that abandons the usual homophonic writing after two or four phrases in favor of an imitative section, followed by a return to homophonic texture. Although the fuguing tune is not a contrapuntal fugue as the name implies, it does have the stylistic feature of the voices entering separately as in a fugue. The imitation, however, is usually free and when strict, as often at the interval of an octave in the first answer as at the fifth.

7. This advertisement ran on July 9 and July 16. Kirkham's book was the popular grammar text of the time.

8. The term *edition* does not appear on any issue until 1850. Each edition presumes that the contents were reset or that new plates were cast.

9. Walter Sutton, *The Western Book Trade: Cincinnati as a Nineteenth-Century Publishing and Book-Trade Center* (Columbus: Ohio State University Press, 1961), 70. Stereotyping employs a plate cast from a plaster or papier-maché mold, on which a facsimile of the page of type is set up by the compositor. When fitted to a block, the plate may be used under the press, exactly as movable type.

10. In her introduction to the new edition of *The New Harp of Columbia* (Knoxville: University of Tennessee Press, 1989), Dorothy Horn remarks, "I once drove to a rural section of Indiana to hear a widely publicized yearly singing in which the descendants of the original pioneers met to recreate the singing school that had played an important part in the lives of their ancestors. What I heard was the most unmitigated musical tripe: songs celebrating the beautiful spring, true love, or whatever, and tearjerkers relating the death of a loved one, all set to the tritest of tunes. On inquiry I found that the original singing school had used the wholly admirable *Missouri Harmony,* but in the 1880s the younger members had demanded something more elegant (I cannot even remember the name of the book used). The number of manuals of the same kind published during the later half of the century indicates that this "genteel tradition" could be found all over the country. Only in the more isolated sections of the Midwest and North and in the conservative rural South did manuals of the older type continue to be popular."

11. For a plausible discussion of Timothy Flint as the amateur, see Shirley Bean, *"The Missouri Harmony,* 1820–1858: The Refinement of a Southern Tune Book," unpub. diss., University of Missouri–Kansas City, 1973, 75–98.

12. After 1845, the firm did less in the line of actual publishing and more in the field of printing and stereotyping, finally becoming successors to Oliver Wells and Company as stereotypers in 1850–51.

13. David H. Shaffer, *Shaffer's Advertising Directory and Cincinnati Directory for 1840* (Cincinnati: J. B. and R. P. Donogh, 1840), 3–5. This advertisement, one of the few to quote prices, is indicative of the variety of printing carried on by Morgan's firm (including Bibles, the works of Flavius Josephus, Hervey's *Meditations,* Bunyan's *Pilgrim's Progress, The New American Readers, The New American Speaker,* Talbott's *Arithmetic,* Kirkham's *Grammar, New American Primers, A Selection of Hymns and Spirtual Songs* by Abbott Goddard, David's *Psalms in Metre,* Miller's *Hymns,* etc.).

14. At one of these concerts held in the Masonic Hall, a $450 rosewood piano was offered as the grand prize. Fine gold jewelry, articles of silver, an accordion, a citron-wood guitar, Jenny Lind's portrait in a gilt frame, a six-octave melodeon piano, were among the lesser prizes offered, with the prizes totaling $765 in value. According to advertisements in the *Cincinnati Gazette,* January 29, 1851; February 4, 1851; and November 22, 1854, the artists were expected to draw a fashionable audience. Police officers were engaged for the evening to insure against any disorder when the prizes were drawn.

15. Among the most famous schools (during the period 1840–1865) for such training were the Cincinnati Normal Academy of Music, the Cincinnati Music Institute, the Louis Ehrgott School of Music, the Cincinnati Music School, the School of Voice Training (directed by B. F. Foley), the Ohio Conservatory of Music, and the Metropolitan School of Music (directed by Winthrop Smith Sterling). An informative discussion of this period is found in Vincent A. Orlando, "An Historical Study of the Origin and Development of the College of Music of Cincinnati," unpub. diss., Teachers College of the University of Cincinnati, 1946, 29.

16. *Cincinnati Gazette,* June 3, 1849, 3. The festival followed the pattern of the German *Saengerfest* held in Bavaria to celebrate the blossoming of the grapes. In 1850, the second *Saengerfest* was held in neighboring Louisville, Kentucky, and in the following year fourteen societies from Hamilton, Newport, Columbus, Cleveland, Lafayette, St. Louis, and Detroit participated in a festival, with a chorus of 247 voices.

17. Ernst C. Krohn, "A Check List of Editions of *The Missouri Harmony*," *Missouri Historical Society Bulletin*, VI (April 1950): 398–99.

18. The family Bible belongs to Mrs. Faxon Small, great-granddaughter of Carden's wife, who resides in Franklin, Tennessee. Information from the Bible has been copied and deposited in the genealogical section of the Tennessee State Library and Archives in Nashville.

19. Davidson County, *Deed Book*, Vols. 1–2, 1836–1839, 23–24.

20. Maury County, *Tax Book*, 1835, 152. The phrase *one white poll* indicates one white male (a son); *two black polls* indicates two black males (slaves).

21. Middle Tennessee District, *Land Grants*, Book 18, Vol. 2, 812; West Tennessee District, *Land Grants*, Book 12, 607, 610–11.

22. David L. Crouse, "The Work of Allen D. Carden and Associates in the Shape-Note Tune-Books *The Missouri Harmony, Western Harmony* and *United States Harmony*," unpub. diss., Southern Baptist Theological Seminary, 1972, 45–46.

23. In 1805, the work was all done by hand. The press operated on the principle of screw pressure. The pressman turned a screw to bring the platen down on the form, which was inked not by composition rollers but by a boy who beat it with inked buckskin balls before the taking of each impression. A stalwart pressman, with the aid of an active boy, could turn out 250 impressions an hour. A complete description of this process may be found in Walter Sutton's "Cincinnati as a Frontier Publishing and Book Trade Center, 1796–1830," *The Ohio State Archaeological and Historical Quarterly*, LVI (April 1947): 117–43.

24. M. Joblin, *Cincinnati Past and Present* (Cincinnati: M. Joblin and Company, 1872), 97. James Lodge came from the office of the *Ohio Republican* in Dayton, joined the firm in 1817, and remained until his death in 1835. Brownlow Fisher became associated with the firm in 1825. Stephen S. L'Hommedieu was placed in the firm in 1821 at the age of fifteen, to learn the printing business.

25. "Our Early Book Supply," *Cincinnati Daily Gazette*, June 12, 1880, 6.

26. Charles Cist, *Cincinnati in 1841: Its Early Annals and Future Prospects* (Cincinnati: E. Morgan and Company, 1841), from a group of advertisements (listing *The Missouri Harmony*) with unnumbered pages following the Appendix.

27. John W. Moore, *A Dictionary of Musical Information; Containing Also a Vocabulary of Musical Terms, and a List of Modern Musical Works Published in the United States from 1640 to 1875* (Boston: Oliver Ditson and Company, 1876), 160.

28. The 1850 Census for Cincinnati also indicates that Warren's parents were born in England. Elizabeth Warren's father was born in France and her mother in England. Names and dates of birth are not given.

29. C. S. Williams, *Williams' Cincinnati Directory and Business Advertiser* (Cincinnati: C. S. Williams—College Hall, 1849–1850).

30. *Ibid.* In the 1853 directory, Warren's same address was renumbered by the city as 486 West 5th, which it remained until 1875.

31. *The Enquirer* (Cincinnati), November 25, 26, 1884, 5.

The Missouri Harmony

THE MISSOURI HARMONY;

OR A COLLECTION OF
PSALM AND HYMN TUNES, AND ANTHEMS,

FROM EMINENT AUTHORS:

WITH AN INTRODUCTION TO THE GROUNDS AND RUDIMENTS OF MUSIC

BY ALLEN D. CARDEN.

TO WHICH IS ADDED

A SUPPLEMENT,

CONTAINING A NUMBER OF ADMIRED TUNES OF THE VARIOUS METRES, AND SEVERAL CHOICE PIECES, SELECTED FROM SOME OF THE MOST APPROVED COLLECTIONS OF SACRED MUSIC.

BY AN AMATEUR.

CINCINNATI:
PRINTED AND PUBLISHED BY PHILLIPS AND REYNOLDS.
LATEST IMPROVED EDITION.
1846

PREFACE.

THE object of this selection is to supply the churches with a competent number of slow and solemn tunes, in unison with the spirit and design of worship. That such a compilation was needed, no person of piety and taste, who has been acquainted with the selections in common use, will deny.

As the great author of our existence has been pleased to favor the human family with devotional exercises, so delightful and becoming, it seems reasonable that they should be encouraged and supported throughout all our divine assemblies. In former times, and under the Jewish dispensation, those expressions of homage were directed by the holy spirit of God, as peculiarly becoming the place where his honor dwelleth. Nay, they seem even to have called on their fellow worshippers to join in this important duty:—*O sing unto the Lord a new song—sing unto the Lord all the earth—it is a good thing to give thanks unto the Lord, and to sing praises unto thy name, O thou most high.*" How astonishing to behold! people who have daily opportunities of opening the sacred volume and contemplating the delightful raptures of the worshippers of old, come into the house of God, and sit, either with their mouths shut, or grinning at some vain and idle speculation, while the devout worshippers are singing the praises of their Redeemer. It was the remark of an eminent writer, too applicable to the present day, that "the worship in which we could most resemble the inhabitants of heaven, is the worst performed upon earth." There appears too much truth in this observation; too often does a disgraceful silence prevail in our churches; too often are dissonants and discord substituted for the charms of melody and harmony. True it is, that there are individuals among us, that providence has not blest with singing faculties; but will not truth oblige the most of us to confess, that the fault rests not in the want of natural abilities, but in a great carelessness and neglect of our own?

This book will be offered to the public in three parts—the first containing all the church music now in use; the second, the more lengthy and elegant pieces, commonly used in concert or singing societies; and lastly the Anthems. Teachers would do well to begin with the first tune in the book, and pursue them regularly as inserted.

None but those who have made the attempt, know how difficult it is to satisfy all. The compiler has had a higher aim; an effort to benefit the church and discharge his duty. He now leaves the work with the serious and candid, and humbly dedicates it to the service of Him

"Whose eye is on the heart;

"Whose frown can disappoint the proudest strain

"Whose approbation prosper even mine."

THE GAMUT, OR GENERAL SCALE.

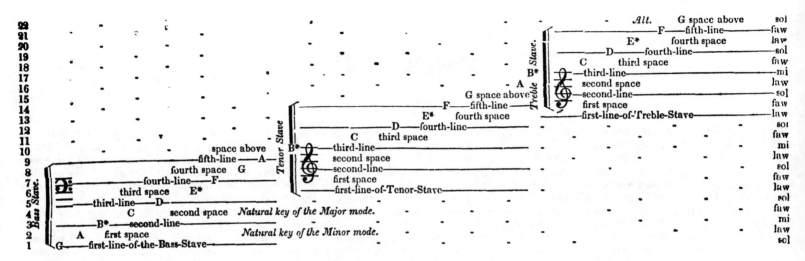

The foregoing scale comprises three octaves or 22 sounds. The F cliff 𝄢 used on the fourth line in the Bass, shows that that line is the 7th sound in the general scale

The G cliff 𝄞 used on the second line in the tenor and treble, shows that that line, in the tenor, is the 8th sound in the general scale, and in the treble (when performed by a female voice) the 15th sound; for if the treble, as well as the tenor, were performed entirely by men, the general scale would comprise only 15 sounds: hence the treble stave is only raised an octave above that of tenor, in consequence that female voices are naturally an octave above men's, and to females the treble is usually assigned. The stars (*) show the natural places of the semitones.

When the C cliff 𝄡 is used, (though it has now become very common to write counter on either the G or F cliffs) the middle line in the counter is in unison with the third space in tenor, (C) and a seventh above the middle line in the bass &c

Three octaves being more than any common voice can perform, the bass is assigned to the gravest of men's voices—The tenor to the highest of men's, and the treble to the female voices; the counter (when used) to boys and the gravest of the female voices.

Two sounds equally high, or equally low, however unequal in their force, are said to be in unison, one with the other. Consequently E on the lower line in the treble stave, is in unison with E on the fourth space in the tenor; and E on the third space in bass, is in unison with E on the first line of the tenor, and an octave below E the lower line in the treble. ☞ See the General Scale. From any one letter in the General scale, to another of the same name, the interval is an octave—as from B to B, D to D, &c.

Agreeably to the F and G cliffs used in the General Scale, a note on any line or space in the bass, is a sixth below a note on a corresponding line or space in the tenor, and a 13th below a note in the treble occupying the same line or space, (when the treble is performed by females.) ☞ See the General Scale. Suppose we place a note on D, middle line of the bass, another on B, the middle line of the tenor or treble, the interval will appear as just stated; and to find any other interval, count either ascending or descending, as the case may be.

EXAMPLE.

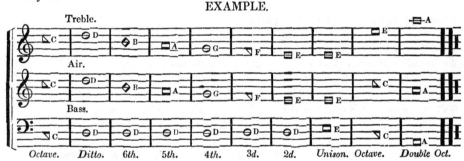

Octave.   Ditto.   6th.   5th.   4th.   3d.   2d.   Unison.   Octave.   Double Oct.

In counting intervals, remember to include both notes or letters—thus in counting a sixth in the above example, D is one, E is two, F is three, G is four, A five, and B six.

In the above example, the notes in the treble and air, are placed in unison with each other. But assigning the treble to female voices, and the air to men's voices, (as is customary,) an octave must be added to the notes in the treble, [as previously observed of a woman's voice being an octave more acute than a man's,] the interval then being the bass and treble—in the first bar, would be a fifteenth or double octave; in the third bar, the note on B in the treble, a thirteenth above D in the bass, &c. Observe that an octave and a second make a ninth; an octave and a third make a tenth; an octave and a fourth make an eleventh; an octave and a fifth, a twelfth; an octave & a sixth, a thirteenth; an octave and a seventh, a fourteenth; two octaves a fifteenth, &c. always including both the first and last note.

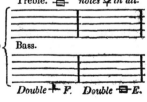

When a ledger line is added to a treble stave, a note occupying it is said to be in *alt*; and when the notes descend below the bass stave, they are termed *doubles*.

TERMS BY WHICH THE DIFFERENT INTERVALS IN THE GAMUT ARE DENOMINATED.

1. An interval composed of a tone and a semi-tone, as from B to D, is called a minor third.

2. An interval composed of two full tones, as from faw to law, is called a third major.

3. An interval composed of two full tones and a semi-tone, as from mi to law, *i. e.* from B to E, is called a fourth.

4. An interval composed of three full tones, as from faw to mi, *i. e.* from F to B, is called a triton or fourth redundant.

5. An interval composed of three tones and a semi-tone, as from faw to sol, *i. e.* from C to G, or from G to D, is called a fifth.

6. An interval composed of three tones and two semi-tones, as from law to faw, *i. e.* from E to C, is called a sixth minor.

7. An interval composed of four tones and a semi-tone, as from faw to law, *i. e.* from C to A, is called a sixth major.

8. An interval composed of four tones and two semi-tones, as from sol to faw, *i. e.* from D to C, is called a 7th minor. [*See next example.*]

9. An interval composed of five tones and a semitone, as from faw to mi, *i. e.* from C to B, is called a seventh major.

Minor Major
7th   7th

10. An interval composed of five tones and two semi-tones, is called an octave, (as has already been observed.) ☞*See examples of the three last mentioned intervals.*

The preceding intervals are counted ascending, or upwards, and the sharps (♯) indicate the places and number of the semi-tones in each. *Note.*—The semi-tones always lie between mi and faw, and law and faw.

OF HARMONY.

Having given an explanation of the different intervals contained in the octave, and the manner in which the parts of music are connected, I proceed to show how they may be used in composition to produce harmony.

Harmony consists in the proportion of the distance of two, three, or four sounds, performed at the same time, and mingling in a most pleasing manner to the ear.

The notes which produce harmony, when sounded together, are called *concords*, and their intervals, *consonant intervals.* The notes which, when sounded together, produce a disagreeable sound to the ear, are called *discords*, and their intervals, *dissonant intervals.* There are but four concords in music—viz: *unison, third, fifth* and *sixth;* (their eighths or octaves are also meant.) The unison is called a perfect chord, and commonly the fifth is so called ; if the composer please, however, he may make the fifth imperfect, when composing more than two parts. The third and sixth are called imperfect, their chords being not so full, nor so agreeable to the ear, as the perfect; but in four parts, the sixth is often used instead of the fifth ; so in effect there are but three concords, employed together, in composition.

N. B. The meaning of imperfect, signifies that it wants a semi-tone of its perfections, to what it does when it is perfect: for as the lesser or imperfect third, includes but three half tones, the greater or major third includes four, &c. The discords are a *second*, a *fourth*, a *seventh*, and their octaves; though the greater fourth sometimes comes very near to the sound of an imperfect chord, it being the same in ratio as the minor fifth. Indeed some composers (the writer of these extracts is one of them,) seem very partial to the greater fourth, and frequently admit it in composition. The following is an example of the several concords and discords, and their octaves under them:

	CONCORDS.				DISCORDS.		
Single Chords	1	3	5	6	2	4	7
Their Octaves	8	10	12	13	9	11	14
	15	17	19	20	16	18	21
	22	24	26	27	23	25	28

Notwithstanding the 2d, 4th, 7th, 9th, &c. produce properly discords, yet they may sometimes be used to advantage, where more than two parts of the same piece of music are written. I would offer as a bare opinion, the following rule for the admission of dissonant sounds:—Where there are two full chords for one discord, they may be admitted, provided a full chord of all the parts immediately follow; "they will then answer a similar purpose to *acid*, which being tasted immediately previous to *sweet*, gives the latter a most pleasing flavor."

ON THE KEY NOTES IN MUSIC.

In music there are only two natural or primitive keys—one of which is cheerful, and called *sharp ;* the other melancholy, and called *flat*. C is called the sharp key, and A the flat key. Without the aid of flats and sharps placed at the beginning of staves, which transpose B, (*mi*,) the centre and governing note, and consequently the keys, no tune can rightly be formed on any other than natural keys. Flats and sharps placed at the beginning of staves, produce what are called artificial keys, and bring the same effect, (*i. e.* place the two semi-tones of the octave the same distance from the key note,) as the two natural keys. The reason why the two natural keys are trans-

flats and sharps placed at the beginning of staves, is, to bring them within the stave and within the compass of the voice. The key notes, or places of the keys, are always found in the last note of the bass, of a correct tune; and is either faw, immediately above mi, sharp key—or law immediately below mi, flat key. The reason why one tune is on a sharp lively key, and another on a flat melancholy one, is, that every third, sixth and seventh, ascending from the sharp key, are half a tone higher than the same intervals ascending from the flat key note. [See the example.]

EXAMPLE OF THE KEYS.

In the Major key, from law to faw, its 3d, the interval is two tones, [a Major third]—from faw to law, its 6th, the interval is four tones and a semi-tone, [a Major sixth]—and from faw to mi, its 7th, the interval is five tones and a semi-tone, [a Major seventh.]

In the Minor key, from law to faw, its 3d, the interval is one tone and a semi-tone, [Minor third]— from law to faw, its 6th, the interval is three tones and two semi-tones, [a Minor sixth], and from law to sol, its 7th, the interval is four tones and two semi-tones [a Minor 7th.]

To prove the utility of removing the key, I will produce one example. Let the tune "*Suffield*" be written on key note A (natural flat key,) instead of E, its proper key—and, besides the inconvenience of multiplying ledger lines, few voices would be able to perform it—the treble in particular.

SUFFIELD—on E, its proper key, from the repeat.   The same on A, the assumed key.

The *mi*, and consequently the *keys*, is removed either by sharping its fifth or flatting its fourth, thus:

BY SHARPS.		
1. A fifth from B mi, its natural place, will bring us to	- - - - -	F
2. A fifth from F mi, will bring us to	- - - - -	C
3. A fifth from C mi, will bring us to	- - - - -	G
4. A fifth from G mi, will bring us to	- - - - -	D
5. A fifth from D mi, will bring us to	- - - - -	A
6. A fifth from A mi, will bring us to	- - - - -	E
7. A fifth from E mi, will bring us back to	- - - - -	B

BY FLATS.		
1. A fourth from B mi, will bring us to	- - - - -	E
2. A fourth from E mi, will bring us to	- - - - -	A
3. A fourth from A mi, will bring us to	- - - - -	D
4. A fourth from D mi, will bring us to	- - - - -	G
5. A fourth from G mi, will bring us to	- - - - -	C
6. A fourth from C mi, will bring us to	- - - - -	F
7. A fourth from F mi, will bring us home to	- - - - -	B

This accounts for the customary rules of transposition, viz:

The natural place for mi is	- - - - -	B
If B is ♭, mi is on	- - - - -	E
If B and E is ♭, mi is on	- - - - -	A
If B, E, and A is ♭, mi is on	- - - - -	D
If B, E, A, and D is ♭, mi is on	- - - - -	G
If B, E, A, D, and G is ♭, mi is on	- - - - -	C
If B, E, A, D, G, and C is ♭, mi is on	- - - - -	F
If F be ♯, mi is on	- - - - -	F
If F and C be ♯, mi is on	- - - - -	C
If F, C, and G be ♯, mi is on	- - - - -	G
If F, C, and D be ♯, mi is on	- - - - -	D
If F, C, G, D, and A is ♯, mi is on	- - - - -	A
If F, C, G, D, A, and E is ♯, mi is on	- - - - -	F

DICTIONARY OF MUSICAL TERMS.

Adagio, signifies the slowest time.
Air, the leading part.
Allegro, brisk—quick.
Allegretto, not as quick as *Allegro*.
Andante, rather slow and distinct.
Affetuosso, tenderly and affectionately.
Adlibitum, or *Adlib.*, at the pleasure of the performer.
Alto, the Counter.
Anthem, a composition of several parts, generally set to sacred prose.
Chorus, signifies that all the *voices* sing on their respective parts.
Crescendo, or *Cres.*, to increase the sound gradually till the strain is ended.
Diminuendo, or *Dim.*, to diminish the sound, directly the reverse of *Crescendo*.
Duetto, or *Duett*, or *Duo.*, a composition in two parts, one voice or instrument, only, on each.
Da Capo, or *D. C.*, to return and end with the first strain.
Expressivo, with expression.
Forte, or *For.*, or *F.*, loud.
Fortissimo, or *Fortis.*, or *F.F.*, very loud and strong.
Finale, or *Fine.*, the last movement of a piece of music.
Fuge, a piece in which one or more parts lead, and the rest follow at regular intervals.
Grave, in a solemn manner, slower than *Largo*, but not as slow as *Adagio*.

Grazioso, a smooth, flowing and graceful style.
Largo, *Lentemento*, or *Lento.*, very slow.
Larghetto, not as slow as *Largo*, &c.
Maestoso, with strength and majesty.
Mezza For., moderately loud.
Mezza Pia., rather soft.
Piano, or *Pia.*, soft.
Pianissimo, or *P. P.*, very soft.
Pastorale, in a tender, soothing and delicate style.
Quartetto, a piece in four parts—one voice or instrument on each.
Quintetto, five parts—one voice or instrument on each.
Solo, a piece of music for one voice or instrument.
Spiritoso, or *Con Spirito*, with spirit.
Stacato, notes stacatoed must be performed very short and bold.
Symphony, or *Sym.*, a passage for instruments only.
Tempo, the regular time.
Trio, music in three parts—one voice or instrument on each.
Verse, one voice to a part.
Vigoroso, with strength and energy.
Vivace, brisk and animated.
Volti, turn over.
Volti Subito, turn over quick.

Obs. 1. Care should be taken that all the parts (when singing together) begin upon their proper pitch. If they are too high, difficulty in the performance, and perhaps discords will be the consequence; if too low, dullness and langour. If the parts are not united by their corresponding degrees, the whole piece may be run into confusion and jargon before it ends, and perhaps the whole occasioned by an error in the pitch of one or more parts, of only one semitone.

2. Each one should sing so soft, as not to drown the teacher's voice; and each part so soft, as will permit the other parts to be distinctly heard. If the teacher's voice cannot be heard, it cannot be imitated; and if the singers of any one part are so loud that they cannot hear the other parts because of their own noise, the parts are surely not rightly proportioned, and ought to be altered.

3. The bass should be sounded full and bold; the tenor regular and distinct; the counter clear and plain, and the treble soft and mild, but not faint. The tenor and treble may consider the German flute, the sound of which they may endeavor to imitate if they wish to improve the voice.

4. The high notes, quick notes, and slurred notes, of each part, should be performed softer than the low notes, long notes, and single notes of the same parts.

5. Learners should sing all parts somewhat softer than their leaders do, as it tends to cultivate the voice, and give an opportunity of following in a piece with which they are not well acquainted: but a good voice may be soon much injured by singing too loud.

6. All the notes included by one slur, should be sung at one breath if possible.

7. All notes (except some in syncopation) should be fairly articulated; and in applying the words, great care should be taken that they be properly pronounced, and not torn in pieces between the teeth. Let the mouth be freely opened, the sound come from the lungs,* and not be entirely formed where they should be only distinguished, viz: on the end of the tongue. The superiority of vocal to instrumental music is, that while one only pleases the ear, the other informs the understanding.

8. When notes of the tenor fall below those of the bass in sound, the tenor should be sounded full and strong and the bass soft.

9. There are but few long notes in any tune, but what might be swelled with propriety. The swell is one of the greatest ornaments to vocal music, if rightly performed. All long notes of the bass should be swelled, if the other parts are singing short or quick notes at the same time. The swell should be struck plain upon the first part of the note, increase to the middle and then decrease or die away like the sound of a bell.

*The organs of a man's voice (or the lungs) is in form somewhat like a tube, about one fourth of an inch in diameter, and possesses power sufficient to divide a note or tone of music into one hundred equal parts.

10. The common method of beating the two first modes of common time is as follows: for the first beat, bring down the end of the fingers to whatever is used for beating upon; for the second bring down the heal of the hand; for the third, raise the hand a few inches; and for the fourth, raise the hand up nearly as high as the shoulder in readiness for the next measure.

For the triple time mood, let the two first be the same as the two first of common time; and for the third, raise the hand a little higher than for the third beat of common time, when it will be in readiness for the next measure.

For the third and fourth moods of common time, and the two moods of compound time, there is just one motion down and one up for each measure; with this difference, for the common time moods there is no resting for the hand; but in compound time, the resting is double the length of the motion.

11. Learners should beat by a pendulum, or by counting seconds, until they can beat regular time, before they attempt to beat and sing both at once; because it perplexes them to beat, name and time the notes all at once, until they have acquired a knowledge of each by itself.

12. While first learning a tune, it may be sung somewhat slower than the mood of time requires, until the notes can be named, and truly sounded without looking on the book.

13. Some teachers are in the habit of singing too long with their pupils. It is better to sing but six or eight tunes at one time, and inform the learners concerning the nature and disposition of the pieces, and the manner in which they should be performed, and continue at them until they are understood, than to skim over 40 or 50 in one evening, and at the end of a quarter of schooling, perhaps few, besides the teacher, know a flat keyed piece from a sharp keyed one; what part of the anthems, &c. require an emphasis; or how to give the pitch of any tune which they have been learning, unless some person informs them. It is easy to *name* the notes of the piece, but it requires attention and practice to *sing* one.

14. Too long singing at one time, injures the lungs.†

15. I have found by experience, that learners will soon know when to sing soft and when strong, if they are led, by the teacher making a larger motion in beating where emphatical words or notes occur, than where others do.

†*A cold or cough, all kinds of spirituous liquors, violent exercise, bile upon the stomach, long fasting, the veins overcharged with impure blood, &c. &c. are destructive to the voice of one who is much in the habit of singing. A frequent use of spirituous liquors will speedily ruin the best voice.*

A frequent use of some acid drink, such as purified cider, elixir of vitriol with water vinegar, &c. if used sparingly are strengthening to the lungs.

16. Learners are apt to give the first note, where a fuge begins, nearly double the time it ought to have; sounding a crotchet almost as long as a minim, in any other part of the tune; which puts the parts in confusion, by losing time, whereas the fuges ought to be moved off lively, the time decreasing (or the notes sung quicker) and the sound increasing as the notes fall in.

17. When notes occur one directly above the other (called choosing notes) and there are several singers to the part where they are, let two sing the lower note while one does the upper note, and in the same proportion to any other number.

18. Flat keyed tunes should be sung softer than the sharp keyed ones, and may be proportioned with a lighter bass; but for sharp keyed tunes let the bass be full and strong.

19. Thirds should not be trilled or turned, lest they become seconds or discords, (though some authors do not confine their compositions to these rules) nor fifths and eighths move together, ascending or descending, lest the parts seem but one.

20. In $\frac{2}{4}\frac{3}{2}\frac{3}{4}$ and $\frac{3}{8}$ the second accent is in common very weak, and in quick time scarcely discernable, except in some particular pieces of poetry to which they are applied.

21. Learners should not be confined too long to "the parts that suit their voices best," but should try occasionally the different parts, as it will tend greatly to improve the voice, and give the person a knowledge of the connection of the counterparts, or of harmony as well as melody.

22. Learners should understand the tune well by note, before they attempt to sing them to verses of poetry.

23. If different verses are applied to a piece of music while learning, it will give the learner a more complete knowledge of the tune, than can be had by confining it always to the same set of words.*

* And likewise applying different tunes to the same words, will have a great tendency to remove the embarrassment created by considering every short tune as a " set piece."

24. Your singers should not join in concert, until each can sing their own part correctly.

25. There should not be any noise indulged while singing (except the music) as it destroys entirely the beauty of harmony, and renders the performance (especially to learners) very difficult; and if it is designedly promoted, is nothing less than a proof of disrespect in the singers to the exercise, to themselves who occasion it, and to the Author of our existence.

26. When the key is transposed, there are flats or sharps placed under each stave: and when the mood of time is changed, the requisite character is placed upon the stave.

27. B, E and A are naturally sharp sounds, and are therefore first flatted, and as F, C and G are naturally flat sounds, they are the first sharped.

28. The appogiatura is placed in some tunes; it may be used with propriety by a good voice, but neither it nor the trill should be attempted by any one, until they can perform the tune well by plain notes; (as this adds nothing to the time.) Indeed no one can add much to the beauty of a piece by using what are called 'graces' unless they be in a manner natural to their voice.

29. There are other characters sometimes used by some authors, as a shake, a relish, &c. but I have reasons for omitting them in this place.

30. All "affectation" should be banished. It is disgusting in the performance of sacred music, and contrary to that solemnity which should accompany an exercise so near akin to that which will through all eternity engage the attention of those who walk in "climes of bliss."

31. The great Jehovah, who implanted in our nature the noble faculty of vocal performance, is jealous of the use to which we apply our talents in that particular lest we exercise them in a way which does not tend to glorify his name.

Q. On what is music written?

A. On five paralel lines ——— including the spaces between them, and those immediately above and be ——— low them, called a stave, calculated to express the degrees or gradations ——— of sound.

Q. Are there not a certain number of sounds belonging to every key note in music?

A. Yes, there are seven, which are expressed by the seven first letters of the alphabet, A, B, C, D, E, F, G.

Q. How many parts belong to vocal music?

A. Four: Treble, Counter, Tenor and Bass.

Q. How are the seven musical letters placed on the Bass stave?

A. Thus:

B	space above
A	fifth line
G	fourth space
F	fourth line
E	third space
D	third line
C	second space
B	second line
A	first space
G	first line

Q. How are they placed on the tenor and treble stave?

A. Thus:

G	space above
F	fifth line
E	fourth space
D	fourth line
C	third space
B	third line
A	second space
G	second line
F	first space
E	first line

Q. How are they on the counter stave?

A. Thus:

A	space above
G	fifth line
F	fourth space
E	fourth line
D	third space
C	third line
B	second space
A	second line
G	first space
F	first line

Q. What have you observed respecting this order of the letters on the staves for all the parts generally?

A. That the order of the letters is the same, though different on the same lines and spaces; for whenever, for instance, G is found A is next, B next, and so on till the whole seven letters occur, and then on the eighth place the same letter occurs again. This eighth place is called an octave, and is considered a unison, or the same sound with the first—so that we may conclude that the whole of music is comprised in seven sounds.

Q. What are cliffs?

A. They are musical characters placed at the beginning of every stave and determine the order of the musical letters on that stave, and generally the part of music written thereon.

Q. Explain then the several cliffs.

A. 1. This character ⨌ called the F cliff, on the fourth line, has heretofore been used only in bass, but is ——— of late often used for the counter, for the purpose of bringing the music in ——— the stave.

2. This character 𝄞 is called the G cliff, is always used in the tenor and Treble, and in modern music, often in the Counter.

---

* As this volume is designed principally for a book of instruction, to be used in schools, the following rules thrown into catechetical order, are intended for mere beginners in music,—the more advanced scholar will find the preceding introduction as still more worthy his study and attention. The compiler here acknowledges himself indeb ed to Mr. "Wyeth's Repository, part second" for many of the rules and remarks contained in this introduction.

3. This character is called the C cliff, and only used in the counter.

Q. By what names or syllables are the seven sounds in music articulated?
A. By those four names—mi, faw, sol, law.
Q. How do you know by which of the names any note is to be called?
A. By first finding where mi, the centre, or governing name is to be found; when that is done, the places, including both lines and spaces, above that of the mi, are faw, sol, law, faw, sol, law, (six places) then comes mi, and consequently the same musical letter again; and below the place of mi, descending are law, sol, faw, law, sol, faw, (six places) then mi, and the same musical letter again.
Q. As it appears then, that mi is the governing name, and determines the names of all the others, pray tell me how you find the place of mi in any tune?
A. The natural place for mi, in all parts of music, is on that line or space, represented by B, but

If B is ♮ mi is on - - - F | If F is ♯ mi is on - - - F
If B and E is ♮ mi is on - - A | If F and C is ♯ mi is on - - C
If B, E and A is ♮ mi is on - D | If F, C and G is ♯ mi is on - G
If B, E, A and D is ♮ mi is on - G | If F, C, G and D is ♯ mi is on - D

Q. But in modern written or printed music books, is there not an easier method of mi, faw, sol, lawing than the one just mentioned?
A. There is: for music is now so written, that the name of each note, is known by its shape—thus, a note when it is mi, is a diamond ◇, when faw, a triangle ▷, when sol, a round ◐, and when law, a square ▣ shape: see the

EXAMPLE.

Q. How many are the musical notes, and what are their names?
A. There are six. viz. the Semibreve, Minim, Crotchet, Quaver, Semiquaver and Demisemiquaver.

The following scale will show, at one view, the proportion one note bears to another

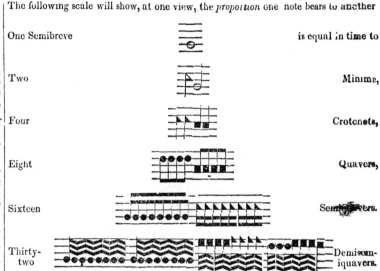

Q. Explain the above scale.

A. The semibreve is now the longest note used; it is white, without a stem, and is the measure note, and guideth all the others.

The Minim is but half the length of the semibreve and has a stem to it.

The Crotchet is but half the length of the minim, and has a black head and straight stem.

The Quaver ♪ is but half the length of the crotchet, has a black head, and one turn to the stem, sometimes one way, and sometimes another.

The Semiquaver ♬ is but half the length of the quaver, has also a black head and two turns to the stem, which are likewise various.

The Demisemiquaver ♬ is half the length of a semiquaver, has a black head, and three turns to its stem, also variously turned.

Q. What are rests?

A. All rests are marks of silence, which signify that you must keep silent so long a time as takes to sound the notes they represent, except the semibreve rest, which is called the bar rest, always filling the bar, let the mood of time be what it may.

THE RESTS.

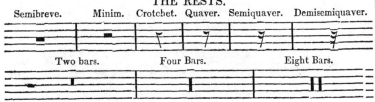

Semibreve.	Minim.	Crotchet.	Quaver.	Semiquaver.	Demisemiquaver.

Two bars.	Four Bars.	Eight Bars.

Q. Explain the rests?

A. The Semibreve or Bar rest is a black square underneath the third line.
The Minim rest is the same mark above the third line.
The Crotchet rest is something like an inverted figure of seven.
The Quaver rest resembles a right figure of seven.
The Semiquaver rest resembles the figure seven with an additional mark to the left.
The Demisemiquaver rest is like the last described, with a third mark to the left.
The two bar rest is a strong bar reaching only across the third space.
The four bar rest is a strong bar crossing the second and third space and third line.
The eight Bar rest is two strong bars like the last described.

Q. Have the notes and rests always the same time?

A. No: Their time varies according to the several modes of time hereafter explained, yet they always bear the same proportion one to another.

Q. Are there not some marks which alter the length of the notes?

A. Yes, the dot ⚫ called point of addition, at the right hand of any note, makes it one half ⚫ longer. See the example.

Also the figure three, over or under any three notes of the same kind, shows that they must be sung in the time of two without a figure.

Likewise a hold 𝄐 over a note shows that it may be held one fourth longer than usual.

Q. What is a ledger line?

A. A ledger line is added when notes ascend or descend a line beyond the stave.

Q. What is a slur and its use?

A. A slur ⌢ over or under a number of notes, or, if made Quavers, Semiquavers, &c. by joining their stems together, shows they are to be sung to one syllable.

Q. Explain the repeat.

A. The repeat  or :S: shows that the music is to be sung twice from it to the next double bar or close.

Q. Explain the use of figures 1, 2.

A. The figures 1, 2 at the end of a strain that is repeated, shows that the note or notes under 1, are to be sung before the repeat, and those under 2, after, omitting those under 1; but if tied with a slur, both are to be sounded at the repetition.

Q. What are meant by notes of Appogiature?

A. Small notes added to the regular notes, to guide the voice more easily and gracefully into the sound of the succeeding notes—these small notes are not to be named.

Q Explain the use of the single bar.

A. The single bar divides the time into equal parts according to the measure note.

Q. Explain the use of the double bar.

A. The double bar shows the end of a strain.

Q. The close.

A. The close shows the end of a tune.

Q. What is meant by syncopation notes?

A. Syncopation notes are those which are driven out of their proper order in the bar, or driven through it, and requires the beat to be performed while such notes are sounding. One or two examples follow, which, with the help of the skilful teacher, will soon be understood by singers of tolerable capacities.

The learner may sing the notes as they stand in the folllowing stave:

THE TIME.

Q. How many moods of time are there in music?

A. Nine: four of Common, three of Triple, and two of Compound.

Q. Explain the four MOODS OF COMMON TIME.

A. The first mood is known by a plain C, and has a semibreve or its quantity in a measure, sung in the time of four seconds—four beats in a bar, two down and two up.

The second mood is known by a C with a bar through it, has the same measure, sung in the time of three seconds—four beats in a bar, two down and two up.

The third mood is known by a C inverted, sometimes with a bar through it, has the same measure as the two first, sung in the time of two seconds—two beats in a bar.

The fourth mood is known by a figure 2 over a figure 4, has a minim for a measure note, sung in the time of one second—two beats in a bar, one down and the other up.

Q. Explain the MOODS OF TRIPLE TIME.

A. The first mood of triple time is known by a figure 3 over a figure 2, has a pointed semibreve or three minims in a measure, sung in the time of three seconds—three beats, two down and one up.

The second mood is known by a figure 3 over a 4, has a pointed minim or three crotchets in a measure, and sung in two seconds—three beats in a bar, two down and one up.

The third mood is known by the figure 3 above figure 8, has three quavers in a measure, and sung in the time of one second—three beats in a bar, two down and one up.

Q. Explain the two MOODS OF COMMON TIME.

A. The first mood of compound time is known by the figure 6 above figure 4, has six crotchets in a measure, sung in the time of two seconds—two beats in a bar, one down and one up.

The second mood of compound time is known by the figure 6 above an 8, has six quavers in a measure, sung in the time of one second—two beats in a bar, one down and one up.

Q. What do the figures over the bar, and the letters *d* and *u* under it, in the above examples of time, mean?

A. The figures show how many beats there are in each bar; and the letter *d* shows when the hand must go down, and the *u* when up.

Q. What *general* rule is there for beating time?

A. That the hand fall at the beginning, and rise at the end of each bar, in all moods of time.

Q. Do you suppose those moods when expressed by figures have any particular signification, more than being mere arbitrary characters?

A. I think they have this *significant* meaning, that the lower figure shows how many parts or kinds of notes the semibreve is divided into, and the upper figure signifies how many of such notes or parts will fill a bar—for example, the first mood of compound time (6 above 4,) shows the semibreve is divided into four parts—i. e. into crotchets, (for four crotchets are equal to one semibreve); and the upper figure 6 shows that 6 of these parts, viz. crotchets, fill a bar. So of any other time expressed by figures.

Q. How shall we with sufficient exactness ascertain the proper time of each beat in the different moods?

A. By making use of a pendulum, the cord of which, from the centre of the ball to the pin from which it is suspended, to be, for the several moods, of the following lengths:—

For the first and third Moods of Common Time, the first of Triple and first of Compound, [all requiring second beats,] - - 39 2-10 *inches*
For the second Mood of Common, second of Triple, and first of Compound, - - - - - - - 22 1-10
For the fourth of Common, - - - - - - 12 4-10
For the third of Triple time, - - - - - - 5 1-21

Then for every swing or vibration of the ball, count one beat, accompanying the motion with the hand, till something of a habit is formed, for the several moods of time, according to the different lengths of the cord, as expressed above.

NOTE.—*If teachers would fall upon this or some other method, for ascertaining and keeping the true time, there would not be so much difficulty among singers, taught at different schools, about timing music together; for it matters not how well individual singers may perform, if, when several of them perform together, they do not keep time well, they disgust, instead of pleasing their hearers.*

Q. What is the use of a brace?

A. The brace links so many staves together as there are parts of the same tune written together.

Q. What are choosing notes?

A. Notes set immediately one after another on the same stave, either of which may be sung, but not both by the same voice. But where there are two or more singers, and choosing notes occur, some may take the upper, and others the lower notes, which increases the variety.

OF THE KEYS

Q. What is meant by the keys in music, how many are there, and how are they known?

A. The key note of every correct piece of music is the leading note of the tune, by which all the other sounds throughout the tune are compared, and may always be found in the last bar of the bass, and generally of the tenor. If the last note in the bass be law, immediately above mi, the tune is on a flat or minor key; but if it be faw immediately above mi, it is a sharp or major key.

There are but two natural places for the keys—A and C. A is the place of the minor, and C the place of the major key. Without the aid of flats and sharps at the beginning of the stave, no tune can rightly be set to any other than these two natural keys; but by the help of these, mi, the centre note, and of course the keys, are removed at pleasure, and form what are called artificial keys, producing the same effect as the two natural ones, i. e. by fixing the two semi-tones equally distant from the key notes. The difference between the major and minor keys is as follows: The major key note has its 3d, 6th, and 7th intervals, ascending, half a tone higher than the same intervals ascending from the minor key note. This is the reason why music set to the major key is generally sprightly and cheerful, whereas that set to the minor key is pensive and melancholy.

NOTE.—*It is of the utmost importance that new beginners in music be taught the difference of the intervals when started from both keys, and this must be done by practice and imitation, for mere directions will not do.*

LESSONS FOR TUNING THE VOICE

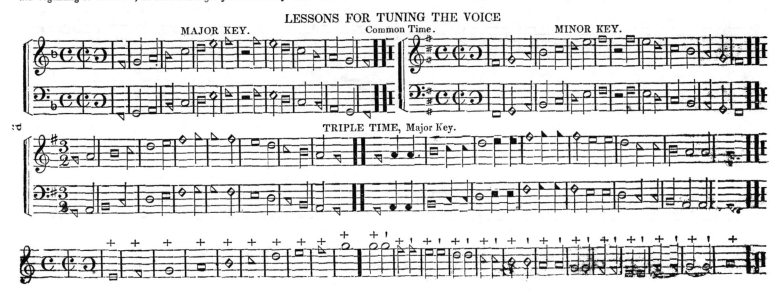

INTERVALS.

NOTE.--- + stands over the usual place of the accent, and over the half accent

PART I

CONTAINING ALL THE PLAIN AND EASY TUNES

COMMONLY USED IN TIME OF DIVINE WORSHIP.

PRIMROSE.   C. M.

Salvation, oh! the joyful sound, 'Tis pleasure to our ears; A sovereign balm for ev'ry wound, A cordial for our fears.

WELLS L M

Ye nations round the earth rejoice Before the Lord, your sovereign king; Serve him with cheerful heart and voice, With all your tongues his glory sing.

ROCKBRIDGE. L. M.

Sweet is the work, my God my King, To praise thy name give thanks and sing; To show thy love by morning light, And talk of all thy truths at night.

Come children, learn to fear the Lord,   And that your days be long,   Let not a false nor spiteful word   Be found upon your tongue.

LENOX. . M

Blow ye the trumpet, blow | Let all the nations know,   The year of Jubilee is come, Return ye ransomed sinners home.
'The gladly solemn sound' | To earth's remotest bound.

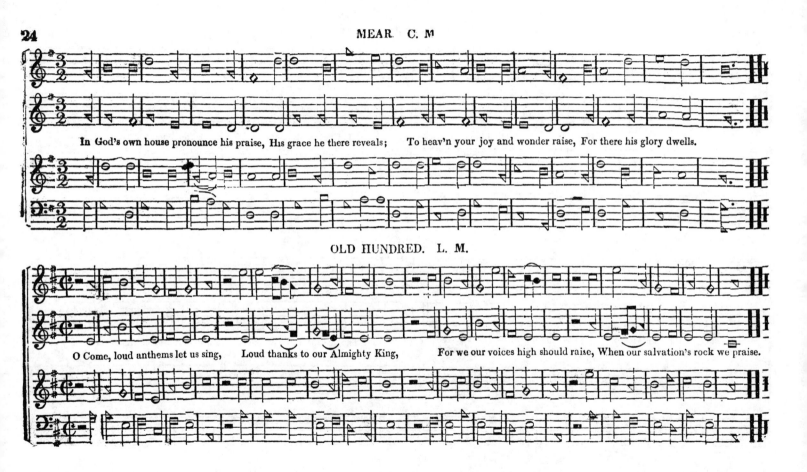

MEAR. C. M

In God's own house pronounce his praise, His grace he there reveals; To heav'n your joy and wonder raise, For there his glory dwells.

OLD HUNDRED. L. M.

O Come, loud anthems let us sing, Loud thanks to our Almighty King, For we our voices high should raise, When our salvation's rock we praise.

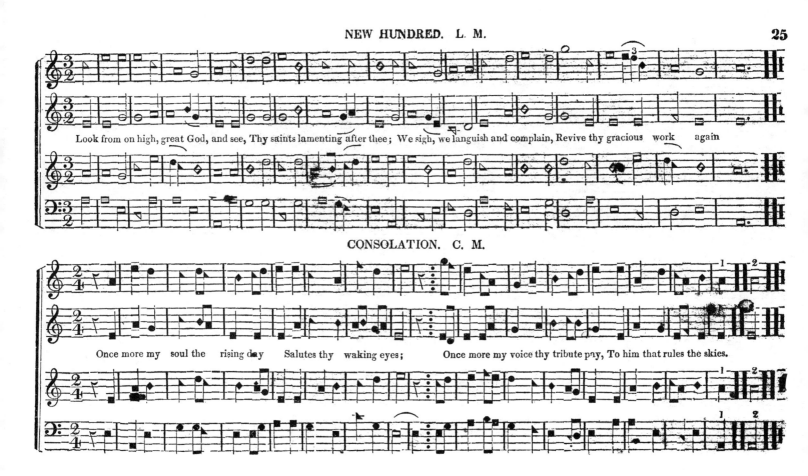

Look from on high, great God, and see, Thy saints lamenting after thee; We sigh, we languish and complain, Revive thy gracious work again

CONSOLATION. C. M.

Once more my soul the rising day Salutes thy waking eyes; Once more my voice thy tribute pay, To him that rules the skies.

WINDHAM. L. M.

Broad is the road that leads to death, And thousands walk together there; But wisdom shows a narrow path, With here and there a traveller.

SUPPLICATION. L. M.

Show pity Lord, O Lord forgive, Let a repent- ing rebel live; Are not thy mercies large and free? May not a sinner trust in thee.

Lord what is man, poor feeble man, Born of the earth at first; His life a shadow, light and vain, Still hast'ning to the dust.

AYLESBURY S. M.

The Lord my shepherd is, I shall be well supply'd; Since he is mine, and I am his, What can I want beside.

NEW ORLEANS. C. M.

Why do we mourn departing friends? Or shake at death's alarms?
'Tis but the voice that Jesus sends To call them to his arms.

Are we not tending upwards too, As fast as time can move?
Nor should we wish the hours more slow, To keep us from our love.

slow, To keep us

GEORGIA. C. M.

Return, O God of love return, Earth is a tiresome place, How long shall we, thy children, mourn Our absence from thy face.

Come humble sinner, in whose breast a thousand thoughts revolve,
Come, with your guilt and fear opprest, And make this last resolve;

I'll go to Jesus, though my sin Hath like a mountain rose;
I know his courts, I'll enter in, Whatever may oppose.

HIDING PLACE. L. M.

Hail sov'reign love, that first began The scheme to rescue fallen man; Hail matchless, free, eternal grace, That gave my soul a hiding place.

SUFFIELD. C. M.

Teach me the measure of my days,   Thou maker of my frame,   I would   survey life's narrow space,   And learn how frail I am.

TENDER THOUGHT. L. M.

Arise my tender thoughts arise,   To torrents melt my streaming eyes;   And thou my heart, with anguish feel Those evils which thou canst not heal.

With cheerful notes let all the earth, To heav'n their voices raise, Let all inspir'd with Godly mirth, Sing solemn hymns of praise.

NINETY THIRD. S. M.

My Saviour and my King, Thy beauties are divine; Thy lips with blessings overflow, And ev'ry grace is thine.

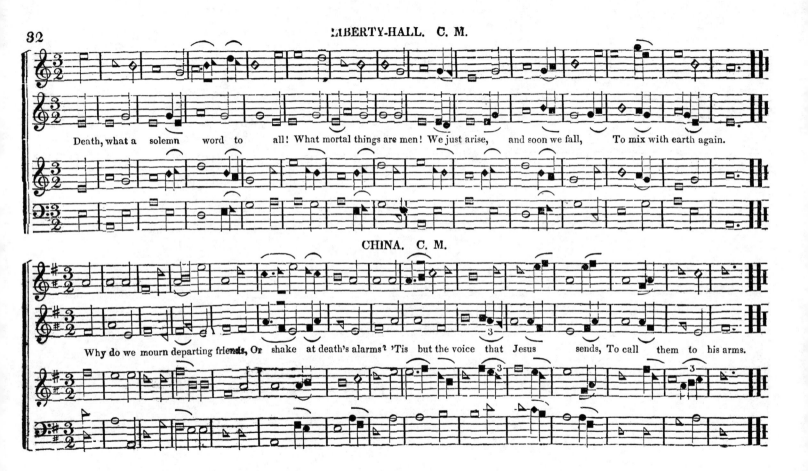

Death, what a solemn word to all! What mortal things are men! We just arise, and soon we fall, To mix with earth again.

CHINA. C. M.

Why do we mourn departing friends, Or shake at death's alarms? 'Tis but the voice that Jesus sends, To call them to his arms.

ST. THOMAS. S. M

Hark, it is wisdom's voice, That spreads itself around; Come hither all ye sons of death, And listen to the wind.

OLNEY. 8s and 7s

Come thou fount of ev'ry blessing, Streams of mercy never ceasing, Teach me some melodious sonnet, [above.
Tune my heart to sing thy grace: Call for songs of loudest praise. Sung by flaming tongues

Praise the mount, O fix me on it, Mount of thy unchanging love.

34

DEVOTION. L. M.

Sweet is the day of sacred rest, No mortal cares shall seize my breast.

O may my heart in tune be found, Like David's harp of solemn sound

SOLICITUDE. 11s.

How firm a foundation, ye saints of the Lord,

What more can he say, than to you he hath said,

Is laid for your faith in his excellent word,

You who unto Jesus for refuge have fled.

O thou in whose presence my soul takes delight, On whom in affliction I call, My comfort by day, and my song in the night, My hope, my salvation, my all.

2 Where dost thou at noon-tide resort with thy sheep,
   To feed on the pasture of love;
For why in the valley of death should I weep,
   Alone in the wilderness rove.

3 O why should I wander an alien from thee,
   Or cry in the desert for bread?
My foes would rejoice when my sorrows they see,
   And smile at the tears I have shed.

4 Ye daughters of Zion, declare have you seen
   The star that on Israel shone;
Say if in your tents my beloved hath been,
   And where with his flock he hath gone.

5 This is my beloved, his form is divine,
   His vestments shed odours around;
The locks on his head are as grapes on the vine,
   When autumn with plenty is crown'd;

6 The roses of Sharon, the lillies that grow
   In vales on the banks of the streams;
His cheeks in the beauty of excellence blow,
   His eye all invitingly beams.

7 His voice, as the sound of a dulcimer sweet,
   Is heard through the shadow of death,
The cedars of Lebanon bow at his feet,
   The air is perfumed with his breath.

8 His lips as a fountain of righteousness flow,
   That waters the garden of grace,
From which their salvation the gentiles shall know,
   And bask in the smiles of his face.

9 Love sits on his eyelids and scatters delight,
   Through all the bright mansions on high;
Their faces the cherubim veil in his sight,
   And tremble with fulness of joy.

10 He looks, and ten thousands of angels rejoice,
   And myriads wait for his word,
He speaks, and eternity, fill'd with his voice,
   Re-echo's the praise of her Lord.

CANAAN. C M.

On Jordan's stormy banks I stand, And cast a wishful eye, } O the transporting, rapt'rous scene,   Sweet fields array'd in living green,
To Canaan's fair and happy land, Where my possessions lie, }   That raises to my sight.   And rivers of delight.

CONQUERING SOLDIER.   P. M.

O when shall I see Jesus, And reign with him above,   When shall I be delivered from this vain world of sin, And with my blessed Jesus,
And drink the flowing fountain Of everlasting love.   Drink endless pleasure in.

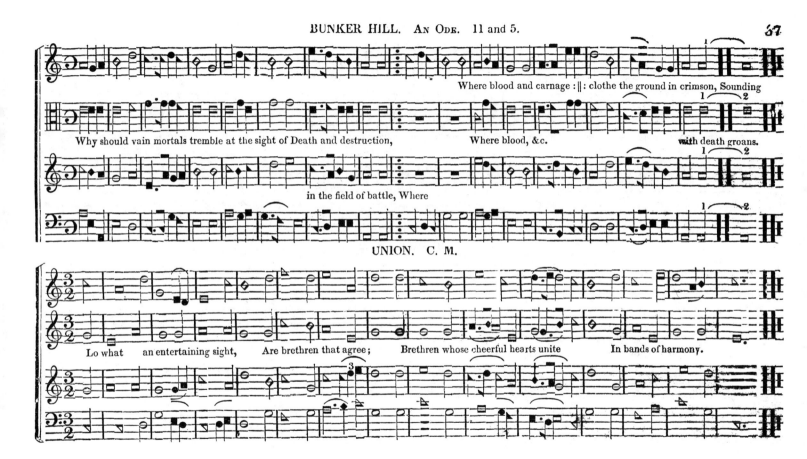

Where blood and carnage :||: clothe the ground in crimson, Sounding

Why should vain mortals tremble at the sight of Death and destruction,   Where blood, &c.   with death groans.

in the field of battle, Where

UNION. C. M.

Lo what   an entertaining sight,   Are brethren that agree;   Brethren whose cheerful hearts unite   In bands of harmony.

SUTTON. C. M.

Behold the man three score and ten, Upon a dying bed, Has run his race, and got no grace, Poor man he lies in sore surprise, No grace I've got
An awful sight indeed. And thus he doth complain

IDUMEA. S. M.

and I cannot recal my time again. My God, my life, my love, To thee, to thee I call; I cannot live, if thou remove, For thou art all in all.

BETHEL. C. M.

Let Zion and her sons rejoice,   Behold   the promis'd   hour; Her God hath heard her mourning voice   And   comes t' exalt his pow'r.

ROCKINGHAM. C. M.

Thus saith the   mercy   of the Lord, I'll be   a   God to thee; I'll bless thy num'rous race, and   they Shall   be   a   seed   for   me.

In vain the wealthy mortals toil, and heap their shining dust in vain;) Their golden cordials cannot ease Their pained hearts or aching heads, Nor fright, nor bribe
Look down & scorn the humble poor, & boast their lofty hills of gain,) approaching death From glitt'ring

SOLEMNITY. L. M

roofs & downy beds. 'Twas on that dark, that doleful night, When pow'rs of earth & hell arose Against the Son of God's delight, And friends betray'd him to his foes.

BRAY. C. M.

Awake my heart, **arise my** tongue, Prepare a tuneful voice, In God the life of all my joys, Aloud will I rejoice. Aloud, &c.

VIRGINIA. C. M.

Thy words the raging winds control, And rule the boist'rous deep, Thou mak'st the sleeping billows roll, The rolling billows sleep, The rolling, &c.

42

ENFIELD. C. M.

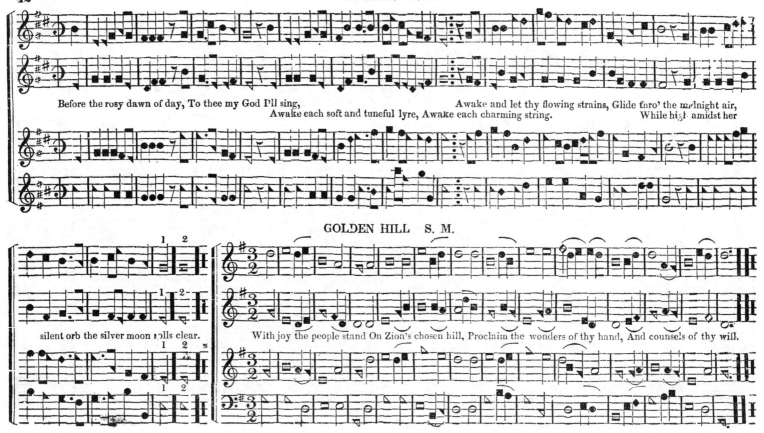

Before the rosy dawn of day, To thee my God I'll sing,
Awake each soft and tuneful lyre, Awake each charming string.

Awake and let thy flowing strains, Glide thro' the midnight air,
While high amidst her

silent orb the silver moon rolls clear.

GOLDEN HILL S. M.

With joy the people stand On Zion's chosen hill, Proclaim the wonders of thy hand, And counsels of thy will.

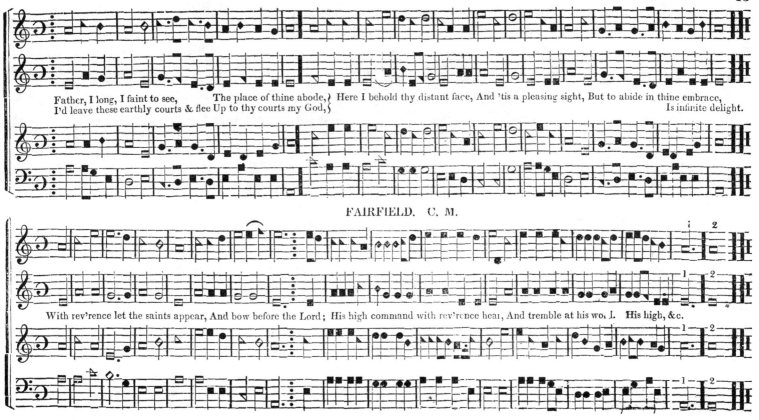

Father, I long, I faint to see,   The place of thine abode, Here I behold thy distant face, And 'tis a pleasing sight, But to abide in thine embrace,
I'd leave these earthly courts & flee Up to thy courts my God,   Is infinite delight.

FAIRFIELD. C. M.

With rev'rence let the saints appear, And bow before the Lord; His high command with rev'rence hear, And tremble at his word. His high, &c.

44

CONDESCENSION. C. M.

How condescending and how kind Was God's eternal son! Our mis'ry reach'd his heav'nly mind, And pity brought them down.

REFLECTION. C. M.

o sleep nor slumber to his eyes Good David would afford, Till he had found, below the skies, A dwelling for the Lord. A dwelling, &c.

O, were I like a feathered dove, And innocence had wings, I'd fly and make a long remove, From all these restless things. Let

me to some wild desert go, And find a peaceful home, Where storms of malice never blow, And sorrows never come.

Death! 'tis a melan- choly day, To those that have no God, When the poor soul is forc'd away, To seek her last abode.

AMANDA. L. M.

Death, like an over flowing stream, Sweeps us away, our life's a dream, An empty tale, a morning flow'r, Cut down and wither'd in an hour.

SALEM. L. M.

He dies! the friend of sinners dies! Lo Salem's daughters weep around; A solemn darkness veils the skies, A sudden trembling shakes the ground.

GLASGOW. L. M.

This life's a dream, an empty show, But the bright world to which I go, Hath joys substantial and sincere, When I shall wake and find me there.

SOPHRONIA. P. M. or 10 and 8

Forbear, my friends, forbear, and ask no more, Where all my cheerful joys are fled? Why will you make me talk my torments o'er? My life, my joy, my comfort's dead-

NINETY FIFTH. C. M.

When I can read my title clear To mansions in the skies, I'll bid farewell to ev'ry fear, And wipe my weeping eyes.

ALBION. C. M.

Come ye that love the Lord, And let your love be known; Join in a song of sweet accord, And thus surround the throne. And thus; &c

AMERICA. S. M.

My soul repeat his praise, Whose mercies are so great; Whose anger is so slow to rise, So ready to abate.

Come thou fount of ev'ry blessing, Tune my heart to sing thy grace; Streams of mercy, never ceasing, Call for songs of loudest praise.

ELYSIUM. S. M.

On the fair heav'nly hills, The saints are bless'd above, Where joy like morning dew distils, And all the air is love, And all the air is love.

HYMN TO THE TRINITY. 6. 6. 4. 6. 6. 6. 4.

Come, thou Almighty King, Help us thy name to sing, Help us to praise! Father all glorious, O'er all victorious, Come and reign over us, Ancient of days.

WINTER. C. M.

His hoary frost, his fleecy snow, Descend and clothe the ground; The liquid streams forbear to flow, In icy fetters bound.

DALSTON. S. P. M.

How does my heart rejoice To hear the public voice,   Yes with a cheerful zeal We'll haste to Zion's hill.

"Come, let us seek our God to-day!"   And there our vows and honors pay.

GREENFIELDS.

How tedious and tasteless the hours, When Jesus no longer I see; Sweet prospects, sweet birds, and sweet flow'rs Have all lost their sweetness to me.
The midsummer sun shines but dim, The fields strive in vain to look gay; But when I am happy in Him, December's as pleasant as May.

False are the men of high degree, The baser sort are vanity: Laid in a balance both appear, Light as a puff of empty air.

WESLEY.   C. M.

With inward pain my heart strings sound, My soul dissolves away. Dear sov'reign whirl the seasons round, And bring :||: :||: the promis'd day.

While beauty and youth are in their full prime, And folly and fashion affect our whole time; O let not the phantom our wishes engage,
Let us live so in youth that we blush not in age.

2 The vain and the young may attend us awhile,
But let not their flat'ry our prudence beguile;
Let us covet those charms that shall never decay,
Nor listen to all that deceivers can say.

3 I sigh not for beauty nor languish for wealth,
But grant me kind Providence, virtue and health;
Then richer than kings and far happier than they,
My days shall pass swiftly and sweetly away.

4 For when age steals on me, and youth is no more,
And the moralist time shakes his glass at my door;

What pleasure in beauty or wealth can I find,
My beauty, my wealth, is a sweet peace of mind.

5 That peace I'll preserve it as pure as 'twas giv'n,
Shall last in my bosom an earnest of heav'n;
For virtue and wisdom can warm the cold scene,
And sixty can flourish as gay as sixteen.

6 And when I the burden of life shall have borne,
And death with his sickle shall cut the ripe corn,
Re-ascend to my God without murmur or sigh,
I'll bless the kind summons and lie down and die.

JEFFERSON. 8 and 7.

Glorious things of thee are spoken, Zion, city of our God: He whose word can ne'er be broken, Form'd thee for his own abode. On the rock of ages founded, Who can shake thy sure repose.

With salvation's walls surrounded, Thou mayst smile at all thy foes.

VERNON L. M

Come, O! thou traveller unknown, Whom still I hold but cannot see, My company before is gone, And I am left alone with thee; With thee all night I mean to stay, And wrestle till the break of day.

EVENING SHADE. S. M.

The day is pass'd and gone, The evening shades appear;   O may we all remember well, O may we, &c.   The night of death is near.

We lay our garments by, Upon our beds to rest;   So death will soon disrobe us all,   So death, &c.   Of what we here possess.

SICILIAN MARINER S HYMN. L. M.

Moderato.

O turn, great ruler of the skies!   Turn from my sins thy searching eyes!   My mind from ev'ry fear release, And soothe my troubled thoughts to rest.

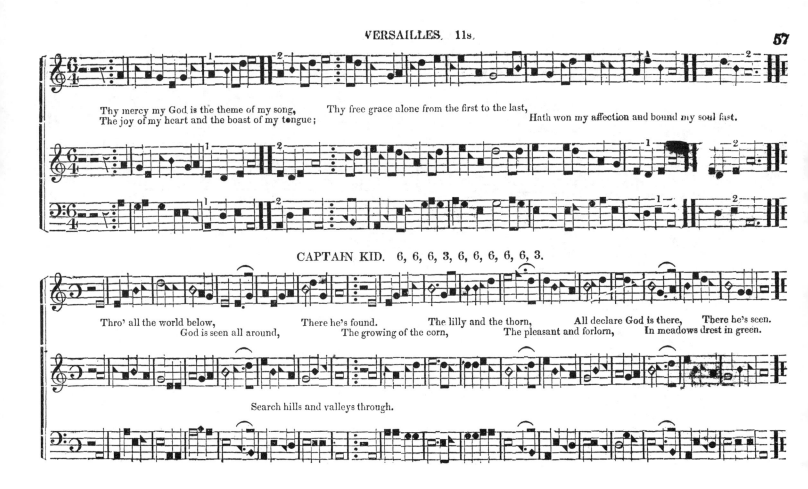

Thy mercy my God is the theme of my song,
The joy of my heart and the boast of my tongue;

Thy free grace alone from the first to the last,

Hath won my affection and bound my soul fast.

CAPTAIN KID. 6, 6, 6, 3, 6, 6, 6, 6, 6, 3.

Thro' all the world below,
God is seen all around,

There he's found.

The growing of the corn,

The lilly and the thorn,

The pleasant and forlorn,

All declare God is there,

In meadows drest in green.

There he's seen.

Search hills and valleys through.

58

GANGES. 8, 8, 6.

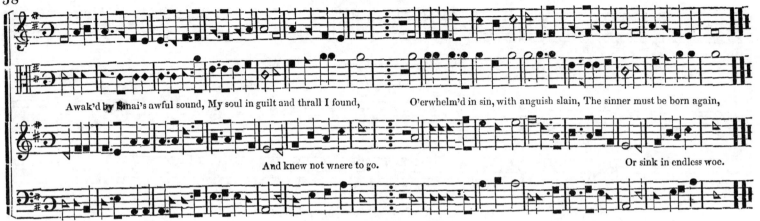

Awak'd by Sinai's awful sound, My soul in guilt and thrall I found,　　O'erwhelm'd in sin, with anguish slain, The sinner must be born again,

And knew not where to go.　　　　　Or sink in endless woe.

2 Amaz'd I stood, but could not tell,
Which way to shun the gates of hell,
　For death and hell drew near;
I strove indeed, but strove in vain,
The sinner must be born again,
　Still sounded in my ear.

3 When to the law I trembling fled,
It pour'd its curses on my head,
　I no relief could find;
This fearful truth increas'd my pain,
The sinner must be born again,
　O'erwhelm'd my tortur'd mind.

4 Again did Sinai's thunder roll,
And guilt lay heavy on my soul,
　A vast unwieldy load;
Alas, I read and saw it plain,
The sinner must be born again,
　Or drink the wrath of God.

5 The saints I heard with rapture tell,
How Jesus conquer'd death and hell,
　And broke the fowler's snare;
Yet when I found this truth remain,
The sinner must be born again,
　I sunk in deep despair.

6 But while I thus in anguish lay,
Jesus of Naz'reth pass'd that way,
　And felt his pity move;
The sinner by his justice slain,
Now by his grace is born again,
　And sings redeeming love.

7 To heav'n the joyful tidings flew,
The angels tun'd their harps anew,
　And lofty notes did raise;
All hail the lamb that once was slain,
Unnumber'd millions born again,
　Still shout thy endless praise.

PISGAH. C. M.

And let this feeble ody fail, And let it faint or die, My soul shall quit this mournful vale, And soar to worlds on high. And

soar to worlds on high. And soar, &c. My soul shall quit, &c.

THE LEPEROUS JEW.

Behold the lep'rous Jew, Oppress'd with pain and grief, Pouring his tears at Jesus' feet, For pity and relief. For pity, &c.

O speak the word he cries,	And heal me of my pain;	Lord, thou art able, if thou wilt,	To make a leper clean.
Compassion moves his heart,	He speaks the gracious word:	The leper feels his strength return,	And all his sickness cur'd.
To thee, dear Lord, I look,	Sick of a worse disease;	Sin is my painful malady,	And none can give me ease.
But thy Almighty grace,	Can heal my lep'rous soul:	O bathe me in thy precious blood.	And that will make me whole.

BOURBON. L. M.

'T was on that dark, that doleful night, When pow'rs of earth and hell arose Against the son of God's delight, And friends betray'd him to his foes.

Before the mournful scene began, He took the bread and bless'd and brake; What love through all his actions ran! What won'drous words of grace he spake.

Slow.

Praise to the Lord of boundless might, With uncreat- ed glories bright; His presence fills the world above, Th' eternal source of light and love.

PLEYEL'S HYMN. L. M

Very Slow.

So fades the lovely blooming flow'r, Frail smiling solace of an hour, So soon our transient comforts fly, And pleasure only blooms to die.

BRIDGEWATER L. M.

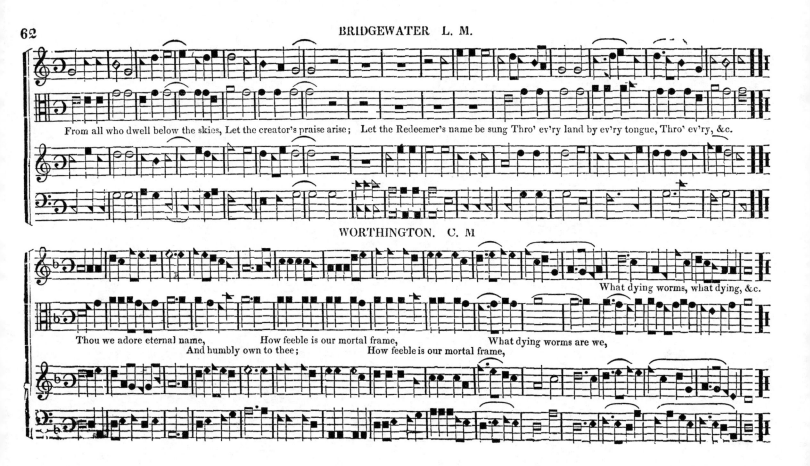

From all who dwell below the skies, Let the creator's praise arise; Let the Redeemer's name be sung Thro' ev'ry land by ev'ry tongue, Thro' ev'ry, &c.

WORTHINGTON. C. M

What dying worms, what dying, &c.

Thou we adore eternal name,
And humbly own to thee;
How feeble is our mortal frame,
How feeble is our mortal frame,
What dying worms are we,

PARIS. L. M

This spacious earth is all the Lord's, And men, and worms, and beasts, and birds: He rais'd the buildings on the seas, And gave it for their dwelling place.

KINGSTON. 8s and 7s.

Agonizing in the garden, Lo your maker prostrate lies!
On the bloody tree behold him, Hear him cry before he dies. It is finish'd! It is finish'd Sinners will not this suffice.

NORTHFIELD. C. M

How long, dear Saviour, O how long shall this bright hour delay!   Fly swifter round ye wheels of time,   And bring the welcome day.

FUNERAL THOUGHT. C. M.

Hark! from the tombs a doleful sound, Mine ears attend the cry: "Ye living men come view the ground Where you must shortly   lie."

O thou in whose presence my soul takes delight, On whom in affliction I call, My comfort by day, and my song in the night, My hope, my salvation, my all.

E BRIDGETOWN. S. M.

Grace! 'tis a charming sound, Harmonious to the ear: Heav'n with the echo shall resound, And all the earth shall hear. And all, &c.

LIBERTY. C. M.

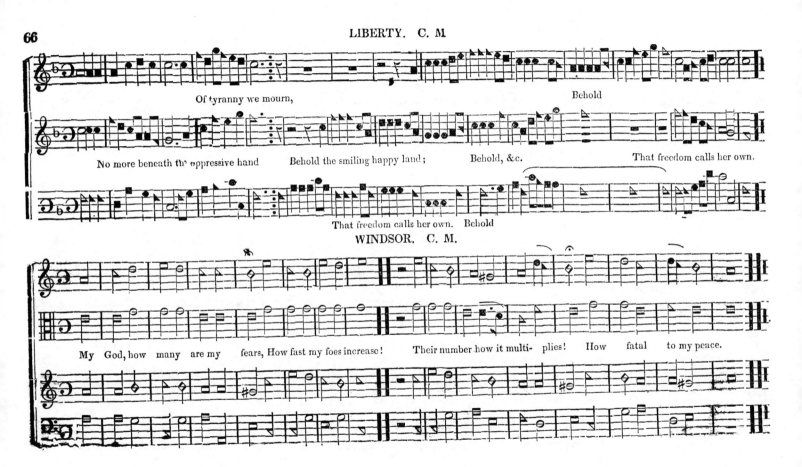

Of tyranny we mourn,   Behold

No more beneath th' oppressive hand   Behold the smiling happy land;   Behold, &c.   That freedom calls her own.

That freedom calls her own.   Behold

WINDSOR. C. M.

My God, how many are my fears, How fast my foes increase! Their number how it multi- plies! How fatal to my peace.

All hail the pow'r of Jesus' name, Let angels prostrate fall: Bring forth the royal diadem, And crown him, :‖: :‖: crown him Lord of all.

WINCHESTER. L. M.

My God accept my early vows, Like morning incense in thine house; And let my nightly worship rise, Sweet as the evening sacrifice.

Sleep, downy sleep, come close my eyes, Tir'd with beholding vanities;   Welcome, sweet sleep, that driv'st away The toils and follies of the day.

MANSFIELD.   S. M.

Let ev'ry creature join to praise th' Eternal God; Ye heav'nly hosts the song begin, And sound his name abroad.   Ye heav'nly, &c.

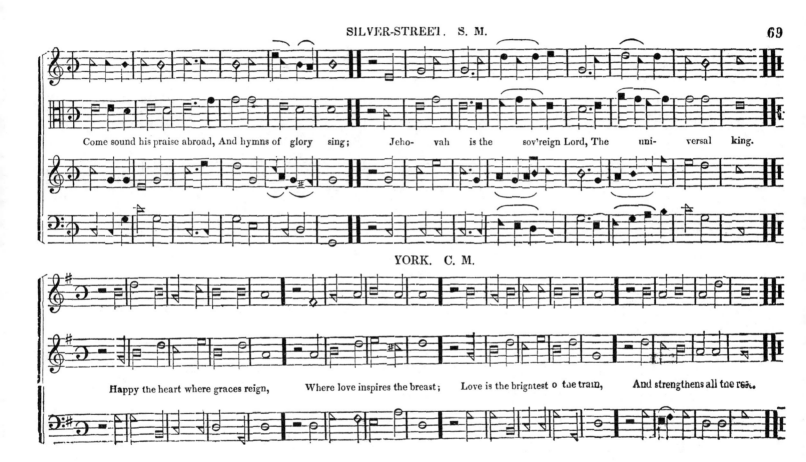

Come sound his praise abroad, And hymns of glory sing; Jeho- vah is the sov'reign Lord, The uni- versal king.

YORK. C. M.

Happy the heart where graces reign,   Where love inspires the breast; Love is the brightest o the train,   And strengthens all the rest.

BATH. L. M.

Life is the time to serve the Lord, The time t' insure the great reward; And while the lamp holds out to burn, The vilest sinner may return

QUERCY. L. M

With all my pow'rs of heart and tongue, I'll praise my maker in my song; Angels shall hear the notes I raise, Approve the song, and join the praise.

ARLINGTON. C. M.

Je- sus, with all thy saints above, My tongue would bear her part, Would sound aloud thy saving love, And sing thy bleeding heart.

LONDON-NEW. C. M.

Let ev'ry tongue thy goodness speak, Thou sov'reign Lord of all; Thy strength'ning hands uphold the weak, And raise the poor that fall.

DEFENCE. S. M.

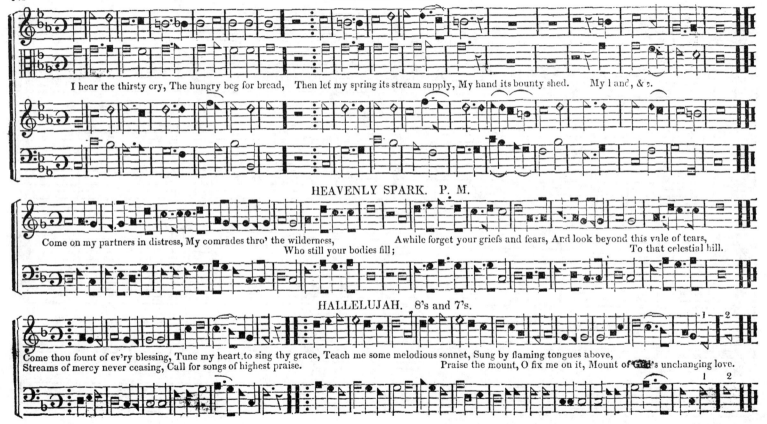

I hear the thirsty cry, The hungry beg for bread, Then let my spring its stream supply, My hand its bounty shed. My land, &c.

HEAVENLY SPARK. P. M.

Come on my partners in distress, My comrades thro' the wilderness, Awhile forget your griefs and fears, And look beyond this vale of tears,
Who still your bodies fill; To that celestial hill.

HALLELUJAH. 8's and 7's.

Come thou fount of ev'ry blessing, Tune my heart to sing thy grace, Teach me some melodious sonnet, Sung by flaming tongues above,
Streams of mercy never ceasing, Call for songs of highest praise. Praise the mount, O fix me on it, Mount of God's unchanging love.

PART II.

CONTAINING THE MORE LENGTHY AND ELEGANT PIECES

COMMONLY USED IN CONCERT, OR SINGING SOCIETIES.

FLORIDA S. M.

Let sinners take their course, And choose the road to death; But in the worship of my God I'll spend my daily breath, But in, &c.

Young people all attention give And hear what I do say; I want your souls in Christ to live, In everlasting day.　Remember you are hast'ning on To death's dark

gloomy shade.　Remember you, &c.　　　　　　　Your joys on earth will soon be gone, Your flesh in dust be laid.

Hark, from the tombs a doleful sound, Mine ears attend the cry; Ye living men come view the ground where you must shortly lie.

Ye living men, &c.

While thee I seek protecting power,   Be my vain wishes still'd,   And may this   consecrated hour   With bet-   ter hopes be fill'd.

Thy love the pow'r of thought bestow'd,   To thee my thoughts would soar,   Thy mercy o'er my   life has   flow'd, That mer-   cy   I adore.

There is a land of pure delight, Where saints immortal reign: In-finite day ex- cludes the night, And pleasures banish pain.

Sweet fields beyond the swelling flood, Stand dress'd in living green; So to the Jews old Canaan stood, Whilst Jordan roll'd between.

GREENFIELD. P M.

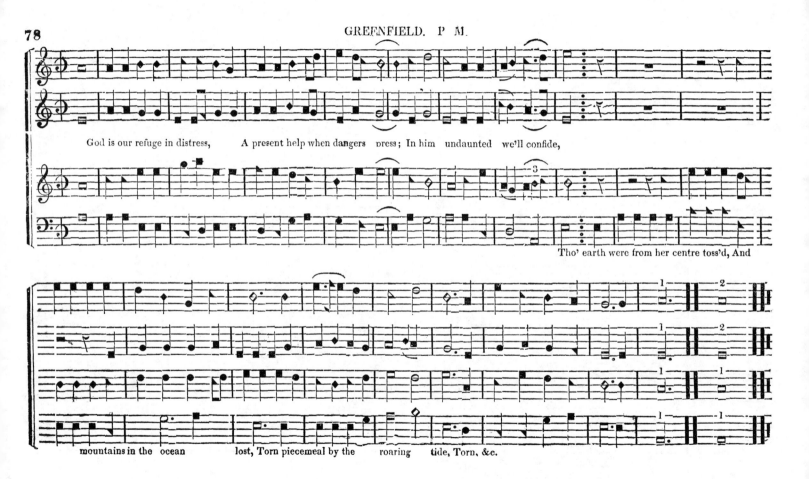

God is our refuge in distress,   A present help when dangers press; In him   undaunted   we'll confide,

Tho' earth were from her centre toss'd, And

mountains in the   ocean   lost, Torn piecemeal by the   roaring   tide, Torn, &c.

Great God at- tend while Zion sings, The joy that from thy presence springs; To spend one day with thee on earth Exceeds a thousand

days of mirth. To spend, &c. To spend, &c.

Early my God without delay, I haste to seek thy face; My thirsty spirit faints away   Without thy cheering grace, So pilgrims on the burning sand.   So

scorching sand beneath a burning sky; Long for a cooling stream at hand, And they must drink or die.

Now let our mournful songs record The dying sorrows of our lord, When he complained in tears and blood, As one forsaken of his God.   The jews behold him

thus forlorn, And shake their heads and laugh in scorn: He rescu'd others from the grave, Now let him try himself to save,

Lord, What a thoughtless wretch was I, to mourn and murmur and repine, To see the wicked placed on high, In pride and robes of honor shine.   But O their end,

their dreadful end, Thy

sanctuary taught me so: But, &c.   On slipp'ry rocks I see them stand, And fiery billows roll below.

I send the joys of earth away, Away ye tempters of the mind; False as the smooth deceitful sea, And empty as the whistling wind. Your

streams were floating me along Down to the gulf of black despair, And while I listen'd to your song, Your streams had e'en convey'd me there.

Thy works of glory mighty Lord, That rules the boist'rous sea, The sons of courage shall record Who tempt the dang'rous way. At thy command the winds arise And

swell the tow'ring   es.   The men astonish'd mount the skies, And sink in gaping graves.

DELIGHT. P. M.

No burning heats by day, Nor blasts of evening air, Shall take my health away;   If God be with me there.   Thou art my sun and thou my shade, To

guard my head by night or noon.   Thou art my sun, &c.

MOUNT SION. S. M.

The hill of Zion yields   A thousand sacred sweets,   Before we reach the heav'nly fields, Or walk the golden streets. Then let your songs abound

And ev'ry tear be dry;   We're marching through Immanuel's ground To fairer worlds on high.   We're marching thro'   :‖:   :‖:

march- ing through

To fairer worlds, To fairer worlds, To fairer, &c. on high. We're marching through, &c.

WILLIAMSTOWN. L. M.

May not May not a sinner trust in thee.

Show pity Lord, O Lord forgive; Let a repenting rebel live; Are not thy mercies large and free?

Hail the day that saw him rise, Ravish'd from our wishful eyes: Christ awhile to mortals giv'n, Reascends his native heav'n;

There the pompous triumph waits, Lift your heads eternal gates, Wide unfold the radient scene, Take the king of glory in.

Behold the judge descends, his guards are nigh, Tempests and fire attend him down the sky. Heaven, earth and hell draw near, Let all things come, To hear his justice.

and the sinner's doom: But gather first my saints, the judge commands, Bring them ye angels from their distant lands.

Thy wrath lies heavy on my soul, And waves of sorrow o'er me roll, While dust and silence spread the gloom; My friends belov'd in happier days,   The

dear companion of my ways, Descend around me to the tomb. My friends. &c.

From all that dwell below the skies, Let the creator's praise arise, Let the Redeemer's name be sung, Thro' ev'ry land by ev'ry tongue. Eternal are thy mercies Lord,

Eternal are thy mercies Lord, E- ternal

Eternal truth attend thy word; Thy praise shall sound from shore to shore, 'Till sun shall rise to set no more. 'Till sun, &c.

How did his flowing tears condole, As for a brother dead; And fasting mortified his soul, While for their lives he pray'd. They

groan'd and cursed him on their beds, Yet still he pleads and mourns, And double blessings on his head, The righteous Lord returns.

The Lord descended from above, And bow'd the heav'ns most high; And underneath his feet he cast, The darkness of the sky.

On cherubs and on cherubim, Full royally he rode, And on the wings of mighty winds, Came flying all abroad. And on the wings, &c.

STRATFIELD. C. M.

Thro' ev'ry age eternal God,   Thou art our rest our safe   abode;   High was thy throne, ere heav'n was made, Or earth thy humble

footstool laid.   High was thy throne, ere heav'n was made, Or earth, &c.   Or earth, &c.

Jesus the vision of thy face Hath overpow'ring charms; Scarce shall I feel death's cold embrace, If Christ be in my arms. Scarce snall, &c.

If Christ, &c.   If Christ,   Then while you hear my heart strings break, How sweet the minutes   ro-   ll

How   sweet the minutes   roll,   A mortal paleness on my cheek, And glory in my soul.   And glory in my soul.

ALL–SAINTS NEW.

Oh! if my Lord would come and meet, My soul would stretch her wings in haste, Fly fearless through death's iron gate, Nor feel the terrors   as   she

past.   Jesus can make a dying bed feel soft as downy pillows are. While on his breast I lean, While on his

Jesus, &c.   While, &c.

Jesus can make a dying bed Feel soft as downy pillows are, While on his breast I lean my head,   And breathe my life out sweetly

G

breast I lean,   I lean my head, And breathe my life out sweetly there. And breathe,   :‖:   :‖:   my life out sweetly there.   1   2

head and breathe, &c.   And breathe my life out sweetly there.   And breathe,   1   2

While on his breast I lean,   I lean, &c.

SHERBURNE C. M

While shepherds watch'd their flocks by night All seated on the ground ; The angel of the Lord came down, And glory snone around.

And glory, &c.   The angel of the Lord, &c.

My soul, thy great Creator praise,   While cloth'd in his celestial rays;   He in full majesty appears,   And like a robe his glory wears.

The heav'ns are for his curtains spread; The unfathom'd deep he makes his bed; Clouds are his chariot when he flies On winged storms across the skies.

When shall thy lovely face be seen? When shall our eyes behold our God? What length of distance lies between? And hills of guilt, a heavy load. Our mouths are

ages of delay, And slowly ev'ry moment wears: Fly winged time and roll away Those tedious rounds of sluggish years. Fly winged time

Fly winged time and roll away, and ro - - - - - - - - ll and ro - - - - ll and ro - - ll away those tedious rounds of sluggish years.

and roll away, and ro - - - - - - - ll and ro - - - - - - ll and ro - - - ll away those tedious rounds, &c.

BABYLONIAN CAPTIVITY. P. M.

Along the banks where Babel's current flows, Our captive bands in deep despondence stray'd, While Zion's fall in sad remembrance rose,
Her friends, her children mingled with the dead.

JERUSALEM. L. M.

This life's a dream, an empty show; But the bright world to which I go, Hath joys substantial and sincere, When shall I wake, When shall I wake

and find me there? O glorious hour! :||: O blest abode! I shall be near and like my God; And flesh and

the hand is thine, Their hope and por-, Their hope and portion lie below; 'Tis all the happiness they know; 'Tis all they

sin no more control The sacred pleasures, :||: :||: of the soul. My flesh shall slumber in the ground

seek; they take their shares, And leave the rest :||: :||: among their heirs. What sinners value I resign,

Till the last trumpet's joyful sound; Then burst the chains with sweet surprise, And in my Saviour's image rise. And in

Lord 'tis enough that thou art mine; I sha - - - ll behold thy blissful face And stand complete in righteousness! And stand

Thou great and sov'reign Lord of all, Whom heav'nly hosts obey; Around whose throne dread thunders roll, And livid lightnings play.

Around whose   pla - - - - - y   play,   Around whose

LIVONIA. L. M.

I'll praise my maker with my breath, And when my voice is lost in death, Praise shall employ my nobler pow'rs. My days of praise shall ne'er be past, While life and

thought and being last, Or immortality endures.   My days of praise, &c.

From low pursuits exalt my mind, From ev'ry vice of ev'ry kind;   Nor let my conduct ever tend To wound the feelings of a friend.   Though

golden flow'rs my path should trace, And joys salute me as I pass; Yet may my gen'rous bosom know, And learn to feel an- oth- er's woe.

Let ev'ry creature join To praise the eternal God, Ye heav'nly hosts the song begin, And sound his name abroad.

Thou sun with golden beans, And mo.n with paler rays, Ye starry lights, ye twinkling flames Shine to your Maker's praise. Ye starry, &c.

EXHORTATION. L. M.

Now in the heat of youthful blood, Re- member your Cre- - - a- - - tor God. Behold the months come hast'ning on

When you shall say, my joys are gone.

When you shall, &c.

My soul come medi- tate the day, And think how near it stands, When thou must quit this house of clay,

And fl - - y to unknown lands. And fl - - - y to un- known lands.

110

SOLITUDE NEW C. M.

My refuge is the God of love, My foes insult and cry, Fly like a tim'rous trembling dove, Fly like a tim'rous, trembling dove, To distant mountains fly.

Since I have plac'd my trust in God, A refuge always nigh, Why should I like a tim'rous bird, To distant monntains fly, Why should I, &c.

Hark, the Redeemer from on high, Sweetly invites his fav'rites nigh; From caves of darkness and of doubt, He gently speaks and calls us out. Come my beloved haste a-

way, Cut short the hours of thy delay, Fly like a youthful hart or roe, Over the hills where spices grow.

Death is to us a sweet repose, The bud was spread to show the rose, The case was broke to let us fly And build our happy nests on high.

Then said I, O to mount away, And leave this clog of heavy clay; Let wings of time more swiftly fly, That I may join the songs on high, Let, &c.

Gently he draws my heart along,   Both with his beauties and his tongue: Rise, saith my Lord, and haste away,   No mortal joys are worth thy stay.

The Jewish wintry state is gone, The mists are fled, The spring comes on; The sacred turtle dove we hear Proclaim the new the joyful year.

The son of man they did betray, He was condemned and led away, Think, O my soul, that mortal day, Look on Mount Calvary! Behold him lamb-like

led along, Surrounded by a wicked throng, Accused by each lying tongue, And thus the lamb of God was hung Upon the shameful tree.

Not to our names, thou only just and true,   Not to our worthless names is glory due;   Thy pow'rs and grace, thy truth and justice claim

Immor- tal honors to thy sov'reign name.   Shine through the earth from heav'n, thy blest abode,   Nor let the heathen say, " And where's your God."

TILDEN. L. M.

This life's a dream, an empty show, But the bright world to which I go, Hath joys substantial and sincere, When shall I wake and find me there? When

Till the last trumpet's joyful sound,

Lord

My flesh shall slumber in the ground, Then burst the chains with glad surprise, And in my Saviour's image rise.

Now to the shining realms above, I stretch my hands and glance my eyes;   O for the pinions of the dove, To bear me to the   upper   skies.

There from the bosom of my God,   Oceans of endless pleasures roll;   There would I fix my last abode,   And drown the sorrows of my soul.

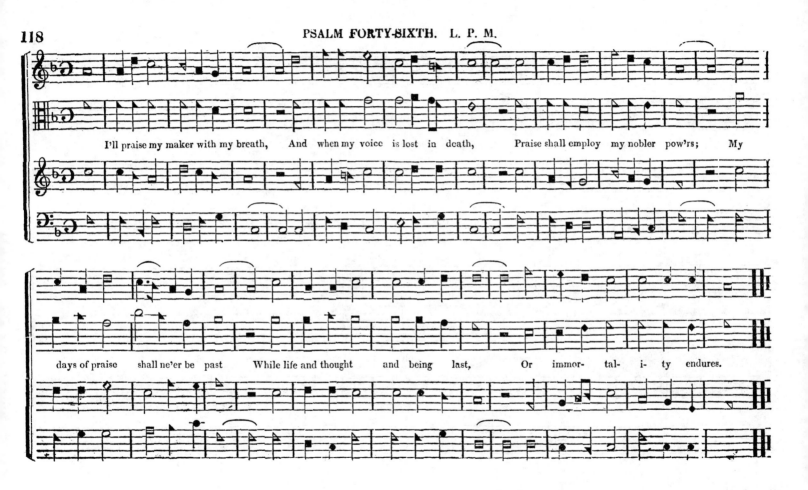

I'll praise my maker with my breath,   And when my voice is lost in death,   Praise shall employ my nobler pow'rs;   My

days of praise   shall ne'er be past   While life and thought   and being last,   Or immor- tal- i- ty endures.

Where nothing dwelt but beasts of prey, Or men as fierce and wild as they, He bids th' oppress'd and poor repair, And build them towns and cities there.

They sow the fields, and trees they plant, Whose yearly fruit supplies their want; Their race grows up from fruitful stocks, Their wealth increases with their flocks.

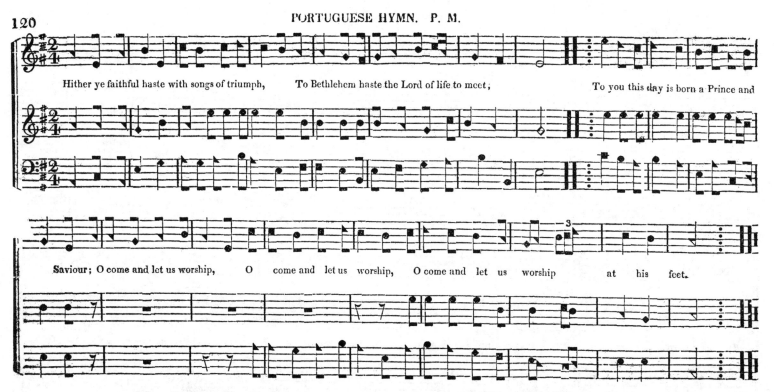

Hither ye faithful haste with songs of triumph,   To Bethlehem haste the Lord of life to meet;   To you this day is born a Prince and

Saviour; O come and let us worship,   O   come and let us worship,   O come and let us worship   at   his   feet.

O Jesus, for such won'drous condescension,   Shout his Almighty name ye choirs of angels,
Our praises and rev'rence are an offering meet;   And let the celestial courts his praise repeat;
Now is the word made flesh, and dwells among us;   Unto our God be glory in the highest.
O come and let us worship at his feet.   O come and let us worship at his feet.

How tedious and tasteless the hours, Since Jesus no longer I see, Sweet prospects, sweet birds and sweet flow'rs, Have all lost their sweetness to me; The midsummer sunshines but dim, The fields strive in vain to look gay, But when I am happy in Him, December's as pleasant as May.

2 His name yields the richest perfume,
  And sweeter than music his voice;
  His presence disperses my gloom,
  And makes all within me rejoice.
  I should, were he always thus nigh,
  Have nothing to wish or to fear—
  No mortal so happy as I,
  My summer would last all the year.

3 Content with beholding his face,
  My all to his pleasure resigned,
  No changes of season or place,
  Would make any change in my mind:
  While blessed with a sense of his love,
  _ palace a toy would appear,
  And prisons would palaces prove,
  If Jesus would dwell with me there.

4 Dear Lord, if indeed I am thine,
  If thou art my sun and my song,
  Say, why do I languish and pine?
  And why are my winters so long?
  O drive these dark clouds from my sky,
  Thy soul-cheering presence restore;
  Or take me to thee upon high,
  Where winter and clouds are no more

122

COLUMBIA. 11s. (Words by Dwight.)

From war's dread confusion I pensively stray'd,

The winds hush'd their murmurs, the thunders expir'd

As down a lone valley with cedars o'erspread,

The gloom from the face of fair heaven retir'd,

Per

A voice as of angels enchantingly sung,

The queen of the world and the child

fumes as of Eden flow'd sweetly along,

Columbia, Columbia to glory arise,

[of the skie

What sorrowful sounds do I hear, Move slowly along in the gale; How solemn they fall on my ear, As softly they pass through the vale. Sweet

Corydon's notes are all o'er, Now lonely he sleeps in the clay, His checks bloom with roses no more, Since death call'd his spirit away.

Sweet woodbines will rise round his feet,
And willows their sorrowing wave;
Young hyacinths freshen and bloom,
While hawthorns encircle his grave.
Each morn when the sun gilds the east,
(The green grass bespangled with dew,)
He'll cast his bright beams on the west,
To charm the sad Caroline's view.

3. O Corydon! hear the sad cries
Of Caroline, plaintive and slow;
O spirit! look down from the skies,
And pity thy mourner below.
'Tis Caroline's voice in the grove,
Which Philomel hears on the plain,
Then striving the mourner to soothe,
With sympathy joins in her strain.

4. Ye shepherds so blithesome and young,
Retire from your sports on the green,
Since Corydon's deaf to my song,
The wolves tear the lambs on the plain;
Each swain round the forest will stray,
And sorrowing hang down his head,
His pipe then in symphony play
Some dirge to sweet Corydon's shade.

5. And when the still night has unfurl'd
Her robes o'er the hamlet around,
Gray twilight retires from the world,
And darkness encumbers the ground.
I'll leave my own gloomy abode,
To Corydon's urn will I fly,
There kneeling will bless the just God
Who dwells in bright mansions on high.

6 Since Corydon hears me no more, In gloom let the woodlands appear, Ye oceans be still of your roar, Let Autumn extend around the year;
I'll hie me through meadow and lawn, There cull the bright flow'rets of May, Then rise on the wings of the morn, And waft my young spirit away.

Mine eyes are now closing to rest, My body must soon be remov'd, And mould'ring lie buried in dust, No more to be envied or

lov'd. No more to be envied or lov'd. Ah! what is this drawing my breath, And stealing my senses away.

O tell me

Oh tell me, Oh tell me,   O tell me n.y   soul is it death,   Releasing me   kindly from clay.   No, mounting my soul shall de-

cry The regions of pleasure and love, My spirit triumphant   shall   fl- - - - - -y.   And dwell with my Saviour   a-   bove.

FORSTER. C. M.

Ye weary heavy laden souls, Who are oppressed sore, Ye trav'lers thro' the wilderness, To Canaan's peaceful shore. Tho'

chilling winds and beating rains, The waters deep and cold, And en- emies sur- rounding you, Take courage and be bold.

'Tis night and the landscape is lovely no more,

For morn is approaching your charms to restore,

I mourn, but ye woodlands I mourn not for you,

Perfum'd with fresh fragrance and

Nor yet the ravage of winter I mourn, Kind nature the embryo blossoms shall save;

O when shall it dawn on the night of the grave.

glitt'ring with dew

But when shall spring visit the mouldering urn,

My gracious redeemer I love, His praises aloud I'll proclaim,
And join with the armies above, To shout his adorable name.

To gaze on his glories divine, Shall be my eternal em-

ploy, And feel them in-ces-santly shine, My boundless in-ef-fa-ble joy

My soul forsakes her vain delight And bids the world farewell, Base as the dirt beneath thy feet And mischievous as hell. No longer will I

1

ask your love, Nor seek friendship more: The happi- ness that I approve, is not within your pow'r.

VERMONT C. M

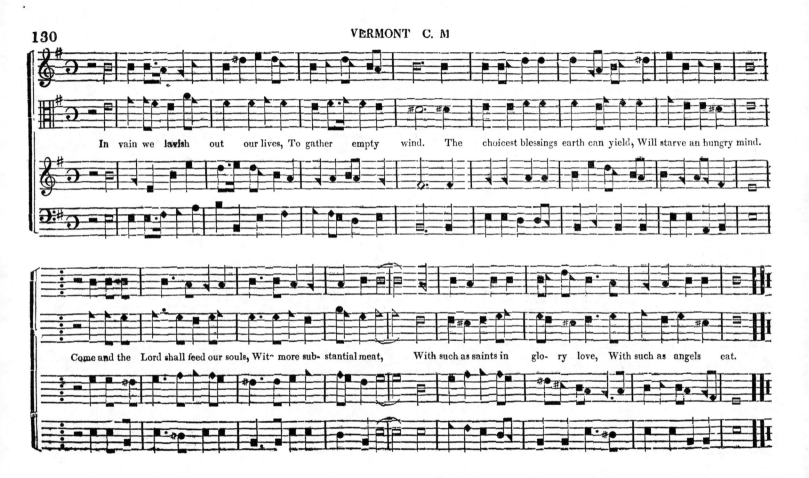

In vain we lavish out our lives, To gather empty wind. The choicest blessings earth can yield, Will starve an hungry mind.

Come and the Lord shall feed our souls, With more sub- stantial meat, With such as saints in glo- ry love, With such as angels eat.

See the leaves around ye falling, Dry and wither'd to the ground; Thus to thoughtless mortals calling In a sad and solumn sound.

Sons of Adam, once in Eden, When like us ye blighted fell, Hear the lecture we are reading, 'Tis alas the truth we tell.

HARTFORD. L. M.

This spacious earth is all the Lord's, And men and worms, and beasts and birds; He raised tne building on the seas, And gave it for their dwelling place.

But   there's a brighter world on high, Thy palace, Lord, above the sky, Who shall ascend that blest abode, And dwell so near his Maker, God.

Stoop down my thoughts that used to rise, Converse a while with death; Think how a gasping mortal lies, And pants away his breath.

Think how a gasping, &c.

WASHINGTON. P. M.

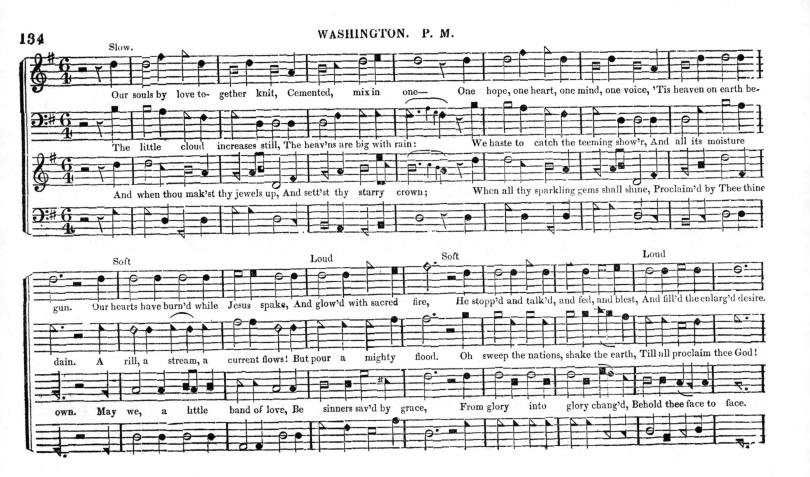

Our souls by love to-gether knit, Cemented, mix in one— One hope, one heart, one mind, one voice, 'Tis heaven on earth be-

The little cloud increases still, The heav'ns are big with rain: We haste to catch the teeming show'r, And all its moisture

And when thou mak'st thy jewels up, And sett'st thy starry crown; When all thy sparkling gems shall shine, Proclaim'd by Thee thine

gun. Our hearts have burn'd while Jesus spake, And glow'd with sacred fire, He stopp'd and talk'd, and fed, and blest, And fill'd the enlarg'd desire.

dain. A rill, a stream, a current flows! But pour a mighty flood. Oh sweep the nations, shake the earth, Till all proclaim thee God!

own. May we, a little band of love, Be sinners sav'd by grace, From glory into glory chang'd, Behold thee face to face.

Cheerful. Eighths. Chorus

He 's God with us, we feel him ours, His fulness in our souls he pours.

"A Saviour!" let cre- a- tion sing, "A Saviour!" let all Heaven ring! He 's God with us, we feel him ours, His fullness in our soul he

pours. 'Tis almost done, 'tis almost o'er, We 're joining those who 're gone before, We then shall meet to part no more, We then shall meet, &c.

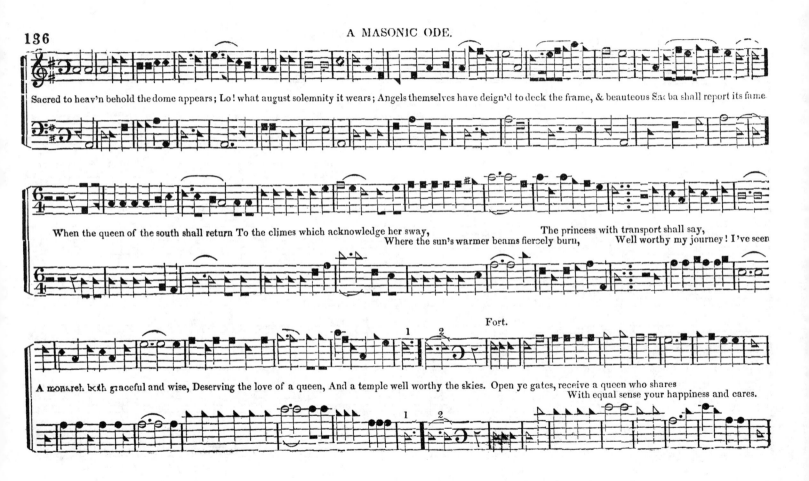

Sacred to heav'n behold the dome appears; Lo! what august solemnity it wears; Angels themselves have deign'd to deck the frame, & beauteous Sacba shall report its fame

When the queen of the south shall return To the climes which acknowledge her sway,
Where the sun's warmer beams fiercely burn,
The princess with transport shall say,
Well worthy my journey! I've seen

Fort.

A monarch both graceful and wise, Deserving the love of a queen, And a temple well worthy the skies. Open ye gates, receive a queen who shares
With equal sense your happiness and cares.

Of riches much, but more of wisdom see;
Proportion'd workmanship and masonry

Oh charming Sheba there behold,
What massy stores of burnish'd gold,

Yet richer is your art. Yet richer is your art.

Wisdom and beauty both combine, Our art to raise, our hearts to join. Wisdom, &c.

Give to masonry the prize, Where the fairest choose the wise.

Pia.   Cres.   Slow.

Beauty still should wisdom love; Beauty and order reign above. Beauty and order reign above.   Beauty   and   order   reign   above.

ODE ON SCIENCE.

The morning sun shines from the east, And spreads his glories to the west; All nations with his beams are blest, Where'er the radiant light appears.

Ye worlds of light that roll so near The Saviour's throne of bliss, Oh tell how mean your glories are, How faint and few compared with his.

We sing the bright and morning star, Jesus, the spring of light and love; See how its rays diffused from far, Conduct us to the realms above.

Its cheering beams spread wide abroad, Point out the puzzled christian's way; still as he goes he finds the road Enlighten'd with a constant day.
When shall we reach the heav'nly place, Where this bright star shall brightest shine? Leave far behind these scenes of night, And view a lustre so divine.

MENDON. 7, 6, 7, 6, 7, 8, 7, 6.

Vain, delu- sive world adieu, With all f creauture good; Only Jesus I'll pursue, Wh. bought me with his blood.

All your pleasures I'll forego, And trample on your wealth and pride, Only Jesus will I know, And Jesus crucified.

Hail! Columbia, happy land,   Hail ye   heroes   heav'n born band, Who fought and bled in freedom's cause, Who fought. &c.

And when the storm of war is gone,   Enjoy the peace your valor won;   Let independence be your boast,   Ever mindful what it cost,   Ever grateful

for   the   prize,   May its altar reach the skies;   Firm   united   let us   be   Rall'ing round our   liberty.

As   a   band   of   brothers   joined   Peace   and   safety   we   shall   find.

God of my life, whose bounteous care First gave me pow'r to move, How shall my grateful heart declare The wonders of thy love.

Thee will I honor, for I stand The product of thy skill; The wonders of thy forming hand, My admi- ration still.

ARCHDALE. C. M.

When God re- veal'd his gracious name, And chang'd my mournful state, My rapture seem'd a pleasing dream,

Piano.

The grace appear'd so great. The world beheld the glorious change, And did thy hand con- fess, My tongue broke out in

unknown strains, And sung surprising grace, My tongue broke out in unknown strains, And sung surprising grace.

DISMISSION. L. M.

I cannot bear thine absence Lord, My life expires if thou depart; Be thou, my heart, still near my God, And thou, my God, be near my heart.

IMANDRA. 11s.

I love thee my Saviour, I love thee my Lord,
I love thy dear people, thy ways and thy word.

With tender emotion I love sinners too,

Since Jesus has died to redeem them from woe.

1 O Jesus my Saviour I know thou art mine,
For thee all the pleasures of sin I resign;
Of objects most pleasing, I love thee the best,
Without thee I'm wretched, but with thee I'm blest.

2 Thy spirit first taught me to know I was blind,
Then taught me the way of salvation to find;
And when I was sinking in gloomy despair,
Thy mercy reliev'd me and bid me not fear.

3 In vain I attempt to describe what I feel,
The language of mortals or angels would fail,
My Jesus is precious, my soul's in a flame,
I'm raised to a rapture while praising his name

4 I find him in singing, I find him in prayer
In sweet meditation he always is near,
My constant companion, O may we ne'er part,
All glory to Jesus he dwells in my heart.

5 I love thee my Saviour, &c.

6 My Jesus is precious—I cannot forbear,
Though sinners despise me, his love to declare;
His love overwhelms me, had I wings I'd fly
To praise him in mansions prepar'd in the sky

7 Then millions of ages my soul would employ,
In praising my Jesus, my love and my joy,
Without interruption when all the glad throng
With pleasures unceasing unite in the song.

Come all ye mourning pilgrims dear, Who're bound for Canaan's land, | Our Captain's gone before us, Our Father's only son,
Take courage, and fight valiantly, Stand fast with sword in hand; | Then pilgrims, dear, pray do not fear, But let us follow on.

2 We have a howling wilderness, To Canaan's happy shore, A land of dearth and pits and snares, Where chilling winds do roar.
But Jesus will be with us, And guard us by the way; Though enemies examine us, He'll teach us what to say.

3 The pleasant fields of paradise, So glorious to behold, The vallies clad in living green, The mountains paved with gold;
The trees of life with heav'nly fruit, Behold how rich they stand! Blow gentle gales, and bear my soul Away to Canaan's happy land.

4 Sweet rivers of salvation all Through Canaan's land do roll, The beams of day bring glitt'ring scenes, Illuminate my soul;
There's pond'rous clouds of glory, All set in diamonds bright; And there's my smiling Jesus, Who is my heart's delight.

5 Already to my raptur'd sight, The blissful fields arise, And plenty spreads her smiling stores Inviting to my eyes.
O sweet abode of endless rest, I soon shall travel there, Nor earth, nor all her empty joys, Shall long detain me here.

6 Come all you pilgrim travellers, Fresh courage take by me; Meantime I'll tell you how I came This happy land to see:
Through faith, the glorious telescope, I view'd the worlds above, And God the Father reconcil'd, Which fills my heart with love.

HIGHBRIDGE L. M.

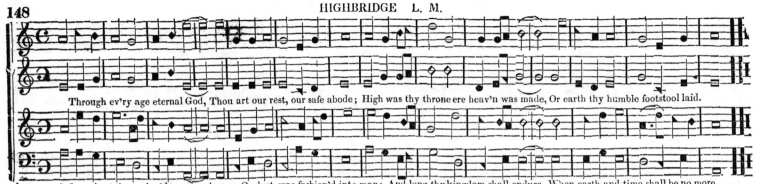

Through ev'ry age eternal God, Thou art our rest, our safe abode; High was thy throne ere heav'n was made, Or earth thy humble footstool laid.

2 Long hast thou reign'd ere time began, Or dust was fashion'd into man; And long thy kingdom shall endure, When earth and time shall be no more.
3 But man, weak man, is born to die, Made up of guilt and vanity: Thy dreadful sentence, Lord, was just, "Return ye sinners to your dust."
4 Death, like an overflowing stream, Sweeps us away; Our life's a dream, An empty tale—a morning flow'r, Cut down and wither'd in an hour.
5 Teach us, O Lord, how frail is man, And kindly lengthen out his span, Till a wise career of piety Fit us to die and dwell with Thee.

LEGACY. 8 & 10

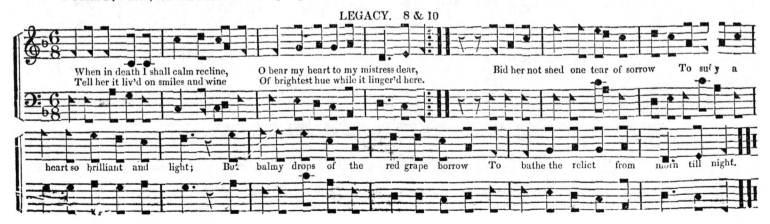

When in death I shall calm recline, O bear my heart to my mistress dear, Bid her not shed one tear of sorrow To suf y a
Tell her it liv'd on smiles and wine Of brightest hue while it linger'd here.

heart so brilliant and light; But balmy drops of the red grape borrow To bathe the relict from morn till night.

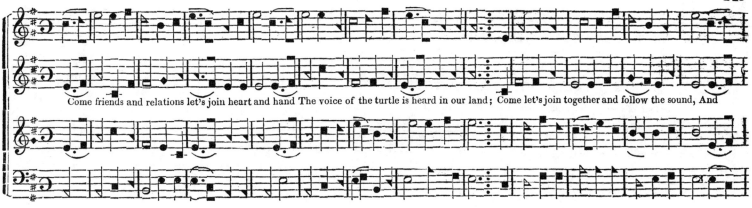

Come friends and relations let's join heart and hand The voice of the turtle is heard in our land; Come let's join together and follow the sound, And

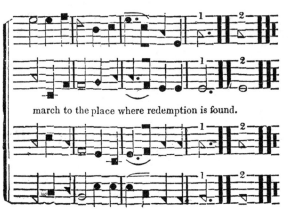

march to the place where redemption is found.

2 The place it is hidden, the place it is seal'd,
   The place it is hidden till it is reveal'd;
   The place is in Jesus, to Jesus we'll go,
   And there find redemption from sorrow and wo.

3 That place it is hidden by reason of sin;
   Alas! you can't see the sad state you are in;
   You're blind and polluted, in prison and pain,
   O how can such rebels redemption obtain!

4 But if you are wounded and bruised by the fal.,
   Then up and be doing, for you he doth call;
   And if you are tempted to doubt and despair,
   Then come home to Jesus, redemption is there.

5 And you, my dear brethren, that love my dear Lord,
   Have witness for pardon, through faith in his blood,
   Let patience attend you wherever you go,
   Your Saviour has purchas'd redemption for you.

150

I'm tir'd of visits modes and forms, And flatt'ries paid to fellow worms; Their conver- sation cloys, Their vain amours and

empty stuff, But I can ne'er en-joy enough Of thy best com-pa-ny, my Lord, Thou life of all my joys.

Bright scenes of glory strike my sense, And all my passions capture; Eternal beauties round me shine, Infusing warmest rapture; I live in pleasures deep and full, In swelling waves of glory; And feel my Saviour in my soul, And groan to tell my

story, And feel my Saviour, &c.

2 I feast on honey, milk and wine,
I drink perpetual sweetness;
Mount Zion's odours through me shine,
While Christ unfolds his glory.
No mortal tongue can show my joys,
Nor can an angel tell them,
Ten thousand times surpassing all
Terrestrial worlds or emblems.

3 My captivated spirit flies
Through shining worlds of beauty;
Dissolv'd in blushes, loud I cry
In praises loud and mighty;
And here I'll sing and swell the strains
Of harmony delighted,
And with the millions learn the notes
Of saints and Christ united.

4 The bliss that rolls through heav'n above,
Through those in glory seated,
Which causes them loud songs to sing,
Ten thousand times repeated;
Goes through my soul in radiant flames,
Constraining loudest praises,
O'erwhelming all my pow'rs with joys,
While all within me blazes.

5 When earth and seas shall be no more,
And all their glory perish,
When sun and moon shall cease to shine,
And stars at midnight languish,
My joys refin'd shall higher shine,
Mount heav'n's radiant glory,
And tell through one eternal day,
Love's all immortal story.

The   Lamb appears to wipe our tears, And to complete our glory,   Then shall we rest with all the blest, And tell the   lovely   story.   To

sit and tell Christ lov'd us well, And that when we were sinners; Heaven will ring, while saints do sing,   "Glory to   the   Redeem-   er."

PART III.

CONTAINING SEVERAL ANTHEMS AND ODES, OF THE FIRST EMINENCE.

LOVER'S LAMENTATION.

That awful day will surely come, Th' appointed hour makes haste, When I must stand before the judge, And pass the solemn test.   Thou lovely chief of all my

joys, Thou sov'reign of my heart, How could I bear to hear thy voice Pronounce the sound, "Depart!" The thunder of that dismal word Would so torment my ear,

'Twould tear my soul asunder Lord, With most tormenting fear.   What! to be banish'd from thy face,   And yet forbid to die!   To linger in   eternal

pain,   Yet death forever fly!   O! wretched state of deep despair, To see my God remove, And fix my doleful station where I must not taste his love.

CLAREMONT.

Vital spark of heav'nly flame, Quit, oh quit this mortal frame, Trembling, hoping. ling'ring, flying,   flying,   flying,   Oh! the pain the bliss of dying.

Cease fond nature, cease thy strife, And let me languish into life, And let me languish into life. Hark! Hark!

Hark! they whisper, angels say, Sister spirit come away.

Hark! Hark! Sister spirit come away, Sister, &c.

Hark! they whisper, angels say, Sister spirit come away, Sister spirit come away. What is this absorbs me quite, Steals my senses, shuts my sight. Drowns my spirit, draws my breath,

Loud.   Soft.

Tell me my soul can this be death?   :‖:   :‖:   The world recedes, it disappears Heav'n opens on my eyes, My ears with

Slow.   Lively.

sounds seraphic ring, My ears,&c.   My ears, &c.   Lend, lend your wings, I mount, I fly, I mount, I fly, O grave where is thy victory? thy

victory, O grave! where is thy victory? thy victory, O death where is thy sting? Lend, lend your wings, I mount, I fly,   I mount, I fly, I mount, I fly, I

fly, O grave where is thy victory? O death where is thy sting? I mount, I fly, I mount, I fly, O grave where is thy victory?   O death where is thy sting?

DENMARK. L. M.

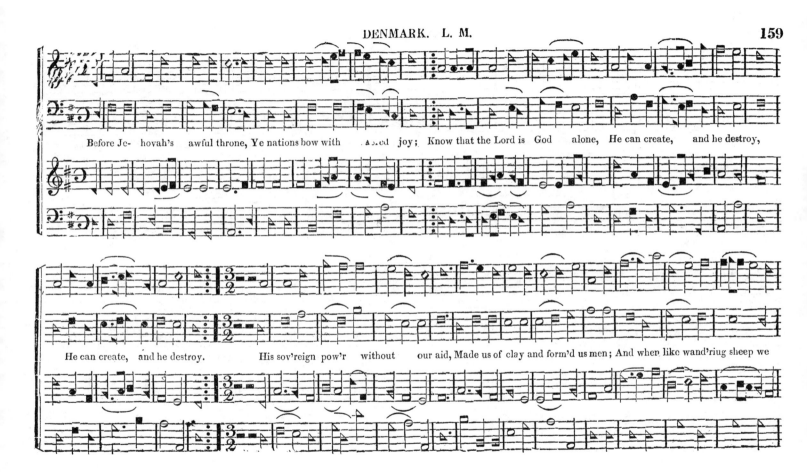

Before Je- hovah's awful throne, Ye nations bow with ...... joy; Know that the Lord is God alone, He can create, and he destroy,

He can create, and he destroy. His sov'reign pow'r without our aid, Made us of clay and form'd us men; And when like wand'riug sheep we

Loud   Soft

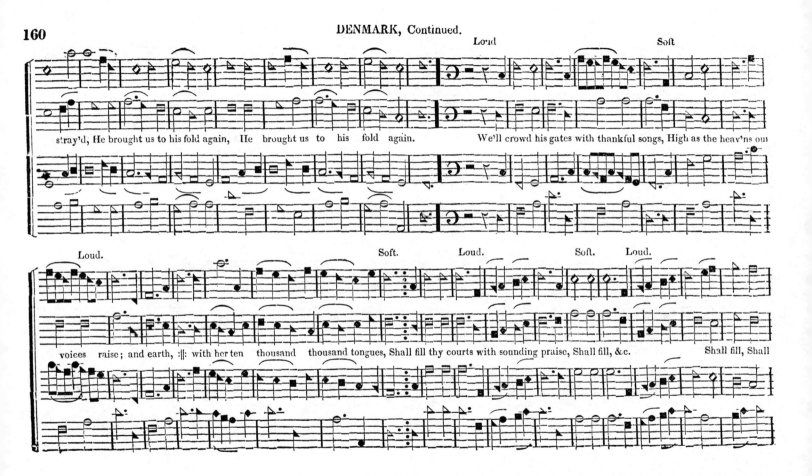

stray'd, He brought us to his fold again, He brought us to his fold again.   We'll crowd his gates with thankful songs, High as the heav'ns our

Loud.   Soft.   Loud.   Soft.   Loud.

voices raise; and earth, :||: with her ten thousand thousand tongues, Shall fill thy courts with sounding praise, Shall fill, &c.   Shall fill, Shall

thy courts with sounding praise.   Wide, wide as the world is thy command, Vast as   eternity,   eter- nity, thy love;   Firm as a rock thy truth shall

stand, When rolling years shall cease to move. When rolling years shall cease to move. When rolling years, &c.

David the King was grieved and moved. He went to his chamber, his chamber and wept; And as he went he went and

said, O my son! :||: Would to God I had di'd, :||: :||: For thee, O Absalom, my son, my son.

The Lord is ris'n in- deed! Hal- le- lujah! The Lord is ris'n indeed! Hal- le- lu- jah!

Now is Christ risen from the dead, And became the first fruits of them that slept, Now is Christ, &c.

164

Hallelujah, hallelujah, halle- lu- jah.   And did he rise?   And did he rise?   And did he rise?   did he rise? near it ye

nations, hear it O ye dead!   He rose, :||: :||: :||:   He burst the bars of death!   :||: :||:   And triumph'd o'er the grave.

Then, then, then I rose, then I rose, then I rose, then I rose, then first humanity triumphant past the chrystal ports of light, and seiz'd eternal

youth. Man all immortal hail, hail, Heaven all lavish of strange gifts to man, Thine's all the glory, man's the boundless bliss. Thine's all, &c.

JUDGMENT ANTHEM.

Hark, hark, hark, ye mortals hear the trumpet Sounding loud the mighty roar, Hark the archangel's voice proclaiming, Thou old time shall be no more!

His loud trumpet, His loud trumpet rends the tombs—Ye dead awake. See the purple banner flying, Hear the judgment chariot roll   roll

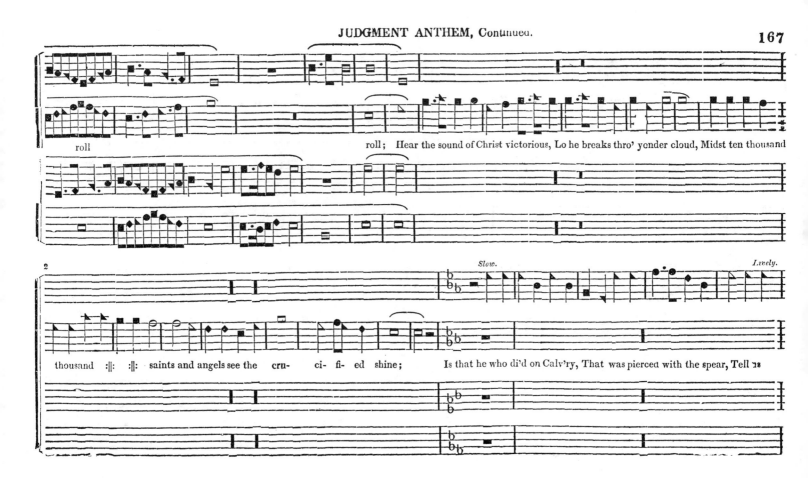

roll

roll; Hear the sound of Christ victorious, Lo he breaks thro' yonder cloud, Midst ten thousand

Slow.   Lively.

thousand :||: :||: saints and angels see the cru- ci- fi- ed shine;   Is that he who di'd on Calv'ry, That was pierced with the spear, Tell us

seraphs, you that wonder'd, See he rises thro' the air, Hail him, :||: :||: Oh yes 'tis Jesus,　　Hallelujah, hallelujah, hallelujah.　　　　O yes 'tis Jesus,

Very lively.　　　　　　　　　　　　　　　　　　　　　　　　　　　　　　　　　　　　　　*Slow and grave.*

Oh, O come quickly, O come quickly, O come quickly,　　　Oh,　　　come quickly, Hallelujah, come Lord come.　　　Happy, happy.

Soft.

mourners, happy mourners, happy mourners,   Lo in   clouds he comes, he comes, View him smiling, Now determin'd ev'ry evil to destroy, All ye nations

Loud.

now shall sing him songs of everlasting joy.   Now redemption long expected, See the solemn pomp appear,   All his people, once rejected, Now shall meet him in the air,   Hallelujah,   hallelujah,   welcome, welcome bleeding Lamb. Now his merit by the harpers, Thro' the eternal deep resonnds.   Now re-

splendent shine his nail prints, ev'ry eye shall see the wound, They who pierced him shall at his appearance wail.

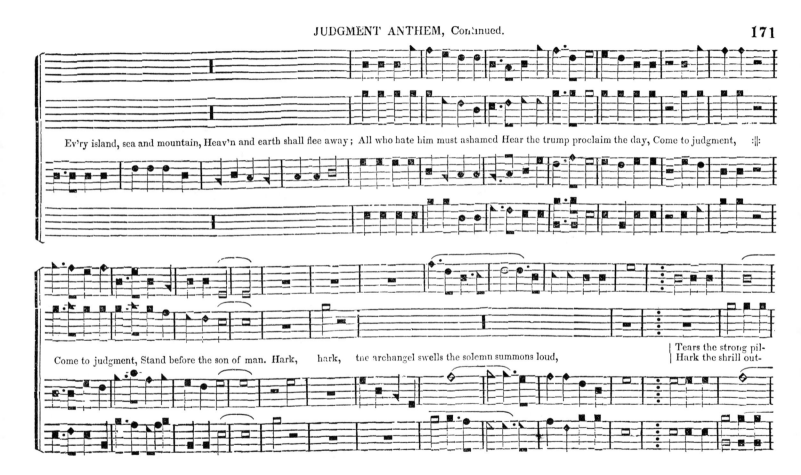

Ev'ry island, sea and mountain, Heav'n and earth shall flee away; All who hate him must ashamed Hear the trump proclaim the day, Come to judgment, :||:

Come to judgment, Stand before the son of man. Hark, hark, the archangel swells the solemn summons loud,

| Tears the strong pil-
| Hark the shrill out-

lars of the vaults of heaven, Breaks up old marble, the repose of princes; See the graves open and the bones arising, Flames all around them.

cries of the guilty wretches, Lively bright horror and amazing anguish Stare thro' their eyelids; while the living worm, Lies gnawing within them.

Brisk.   Very Loud.

See the Judge's hand arising, Fill'd with vengeance on his foes,

Down to hell there's no redemption, Ev'ry Christless soul must go, Down to hell, depart, :||: :||: ve cursed into everlasting flames,

Very slow and Soft. Brisk. Lively and loud.

Hear the Saviour's words of mercy, Come ye ransom'd sinners home: Swift and joyful on your journey,
To the palace of your God. | See the souls that earth despised, In ce-
Joy celestial, hymns harmonious In soft

lestial glories move, Hallelujah big with wonder, Praising Christ's eternal love: Hallelujah, hallelujah echo through the realms of light.
symohony resound; Angels, seraphs, harps and trumpets, Swell the sweet angelic sound; Hail Almighty, :||: Great eternal Lord, Amen.

FUNERAL ANTHEM.

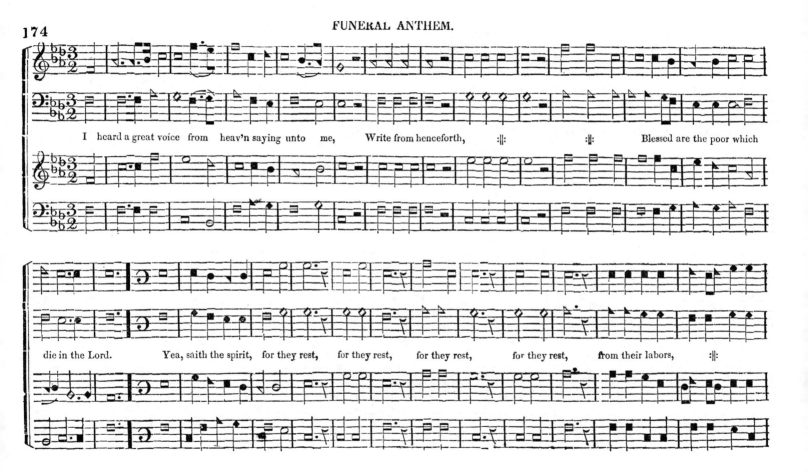

I heard a great voice from heav'n saying unto me, Write from henceforth, :||: :||: Blessed are the poor which

die in the Lord. Yea, saith the spirit, for they rest, for they rest, for they rest, for they rest, from their labors, :||:

from their labors and their works which do follow, follow, follow,   which do follow, follow them.   Which do follow them.

THE ROSE OF SHARON.

I am the rose of Sharon, and the lily of the vallies.   I am the rose of Sharon, and the   lily of the vallies.

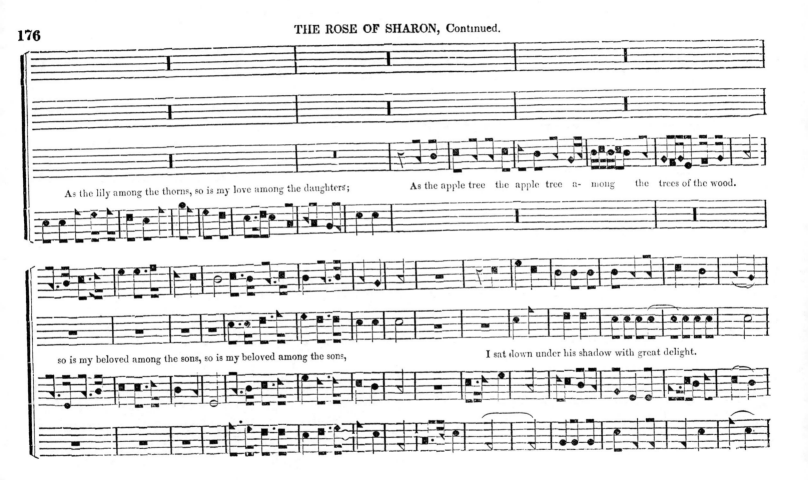

As the lily among the thorns, so is my love among the daughters;

As the apple tree the apple tree a- mong the trees of the wood.

so is my beloved among the sons, so is my beloved among the sons,

I sat down under his shadow with great delight.

And his fruit was sweet to my taste. And his fruit, And his fruit was sweet to my taste.

And his fruit was sweet to my taste.

And his fruit, and his fruit was sweet to my taste, And his fruit, and his fruit, &c. He brought me to the banqueting house,

M

his banner over me was love. He brought me to the banqueting house, his banner over me was love. Stay me with flagons, comfort me with apples, for I am sick, for I am sick, for I am sick of love, I charge you, O ye daughters of Je- rusalem,

By the rose, and by the hinds of the field, that you stir not up, that you stir not up, that you stir not up, that you stir not up, nor a-

wake awake   awake   awake   my love till he please.   The voice of my beloved,   Behold! he cometh,

leaping upon the mountains. skipping,   :‖:   :‖:   leaping upon the mountains, skipping upon the hills.   My beloved spake, and

THE ROSE OF SHARON, Continued.

180

said unto me, rise up, rise up, rise up, rise up my love, my fair one and come a- way. For lo the winter is

past, the rain is over and gone. For lo, &c. the rain is over, the

rain is over, the   rain is   over   and   gone.   For   lo, &c.

THE PRODIGAL SON.

Behold!   behold the wretch whose lust   and wine Have wasted his estate; He begs   a share among the swine, To taste the husks they eat!

THE PRODIGAL SON, Continued.

I die with hunger here, he cries; I starve in foreign lands; My father's house hath large supplies, And bounteous are his hands, And bounteous. &c.

I'll go and with a mournful tongue Fall down before his face: Father I've done thy justice wrong, Nor can deserve thy grace.

THE PRODIGAL SON, Continued.

He said, and hasten'd to his home, To seek his father's love: The father saw the rebel come, And all his bowels move.

He ran and fell upon his neck, Embrac'd and kiss'd his son; The rebel's heart with sorrow brake For follies he had done.

Take off these clothes of shame and sin, The father gives command; Dress him in garments white and clean, With ring adorn his hand.   A day of feasting I or-

dain; A day of feasting I ordain, Let mirth and joy abound,   :||:   My son was dead and lives again, Was lost and now is found   Was lost

I beheld, and lo a great multitude which no man could number, Thousands of thousands, and ten times thousands, Thousands, &c.

Thousands of thousands, and ten times thousands, Thousands, &c. Stood before the Lamb, and they had palms in their

hands, and they cease not day nor night, saying, Holy,   holy,   holy,   holy,   holy,   Lord God Almighty,   was, and is, and

is to come. Which was, &c.   And I heard a mighty angel   fly- - - - - ing thro' the midst of heav'n.

crying with a loud voice, wo, wo, wo, wo, Be unto the earth by reason of the trumpet which is

yet to sound. And when the last trumpet sounded, the great men and nobles, rich men and poor, bond and free, gathered themselves together and   cried   to the rocks and mountains to   fall   upon   them and   hide them   from the   face of   Him nat sitteth   on the throne,

For the great day of the   Lord is   come, and who shall be a-   ble to   stand.   And   who   shall   be   able   to   stand.

Our Lord is risen from the dead, Our Je sus has gone up on high: The pow'rs of hell are captive led,

Dragg'd to the portals of the sky. The pow'rs, &c. Dragg'd, &c. Dragg'd' &c.

Sym.   Loud.

There his triumphal   chariot waits,   And   angels   chant   the

solemn   lay,   Lift up your heads   ye heav'nly   gates,   Ye   ever   lasting   doors give   way.   Lift up, &c.

Sym.

Ye everlasting, &c.

SOLO.

Loose all your bars of massy light, And wide unfold th' etherial scene, He claims these mansions as his right, Receive the king of glory in. He

Sym.

claims, &c. Receive, &c. Receive, &c.

Loose all your bars of massy light, And wide unfold th' etherial scene; He claims these mansions as his right, Receive the king of glory

in. He claims, &c.   Receive, &c.   Receive, &c.

Loud.

Who is the king of glory; who, who, Who is the king of glory, who, The Lord who all his foes o'ercame, The world, sin, death and hell, o'er

threw, And Jesus is the conqueror's name.   And Jesus, &c.   And Jesus, &c.

N

Lo! his triumphal chariot waits, And angels   chant the solemn lay.   Lift up your heads ye heavenly gates,   Ye ev - er - lasting doors give

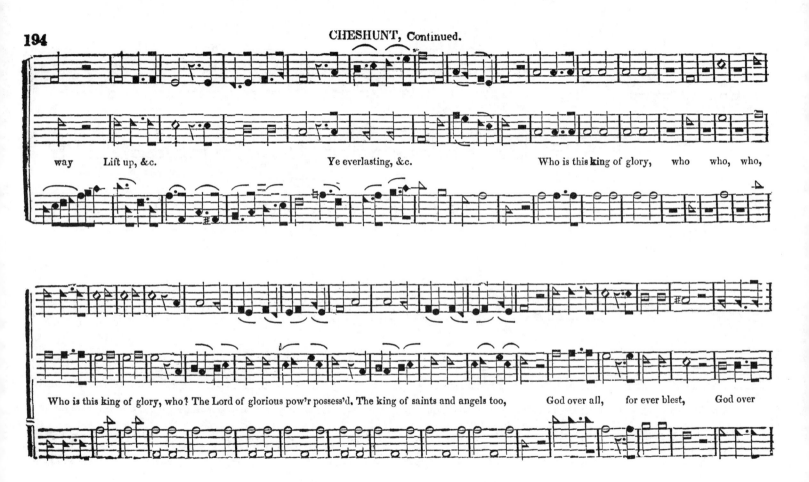

way   Lift up, &c.   Ye everlasting, &c.   Who is this king of glory,   who   who, who,

Who is this king of glory, who? The Lord of glorious pow'r possess'd. The king of saints and angels too,   God over all,   for ever blest,   God over

all for- ever   blest.   God, &c.   God over all, for- ev- er blest, for- ev- er blest.

NEW YORK ANTHEM,
Soft. Slow.

Increase.

Vital   spark of heav'nly flame, Quit,   O quit   this mortal frame, Tremoling, hoping, ling'ring,   flying,   O the pain, the bliss of

sorbs me quite, Steals my senses, shuts my sight, Drowns my spirit, draws my breath, Tell me, my soul, can this be death? Tell me, my soul, can

this be death? The world recedes, it disappears, Heav'n opens on my eyes, my ears With sounds seraphic ring.

Lend, lend your wings, I mount, I fly,

O grave where

198

is **thy** victory! O grave,

O death where is thy sting!

Lend, lend your wings, I mount, I fly

O grave, O death,

O grave where is thy

victory, thy victory! O grave thy O death O death

I mount, I fly,

Lend, lend your wings,

Slow.

Where is thy sting.

mount, I fly, O grave where is thy victory! thy victory! O death, O death,

MOUNT PLEASANT. C. M.

There is a house not made with hands, Eternal, and on high, And here my spirit waiting stands, 'Till God shall bid it fly.

And here

200

And   And   fly

And here   'Till   'Till   fly   fly   fly

'Till   'Till   fly   fly   fly   fly

'Till   And here   fly   fly

SUPPLEMENT

TO

THE MISSOURI HARMONY;

CONTAINING TWENTY-THREE CHOICE TUNES OF THE VARIOUS METRES, ONE ANTHEM, TWO SET PIECES, ONE DUETT, ONE SONG AND ONE SHORT CHORUS. (THE DUETT AND SACRED SONG ARE ARRANGED FOR THE ORGAN OR PIANO FORTE,) SELECTED FROM SOME OF THE MOST APPROVED COLLECTIONS OF SACRED MUSIC

BY AN AMATEUR.

SHIRLAND. S. M.

He leads me to the place, where heav'nly pastures grow; Where liv-ing wa-ters gent-ly pass, And full salvation flows.

CRANBROOK, S. M.   Hymn 92, Dwight's Selection.   T. CLARK.

Grace 'tis a charming sound, Harmonious to the ear, Heav'n with the echo shall resound, Heav'n with the echo shall re-

Heav'n with the echo, &c. the echo shall re-

Grace 'tis a charming sound, Harmonious to the ear, Heav'n with the echo shall resound, Heav'n with the echo shall re-

Heav'n with the echo &c. the echo shall re-

sound   And all the earth shall hear, And all the earth shall hear, And all the earth shall hear.

sound,   And all the earth shall hear, And all the earth shall hear, And all the earth shall hear.

sound. And all the earth shall hear, And all the earth shall hear, And all the earth shall hear.

BRADLEY. S. M.   Psalm 117, Dr. Watts.   3

Thy name, Al - mighty Lord, Shall sound through distant lands, Thy name, Almighty Lord, Shall sound through distant lands,

Great is thy grace, and sure thy word, Great is thy grace, and sure thy word, Thy truth for - ev - er stands.

N B. The above Pia. passage, to be sung as a Trio

OVERTON. C. M. Hymn 72, 2d Book Dr. Watts. T. CLARK.

Sweet to rejoice in live - ly hope, That when my change shall come, Angels will hover, Angels will hover, Angels will hover

And waft my spirit home.

round my bed, And waft my spirit home; Angels will hover round my bed, And waft my spirit home.

And wa — — — ft my spirit home.

And wa — ft my spirit home.

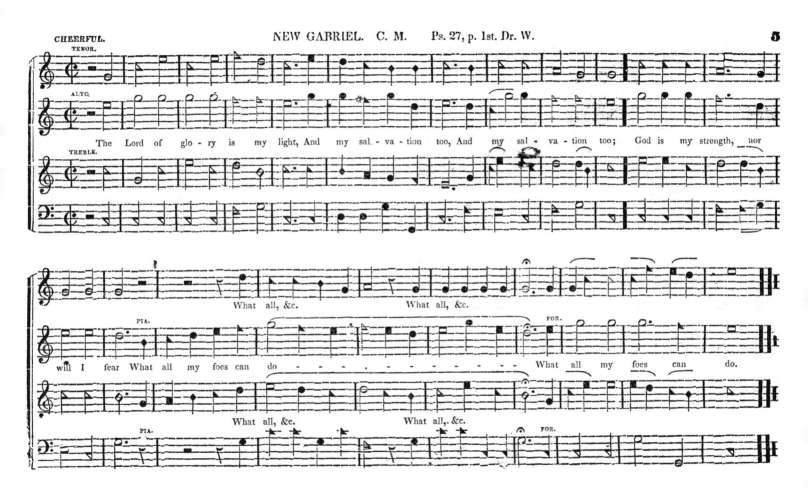

The Lord of glo - ry is my light, And my sal - va - tion too, And my sal - va - tion too; God is my strength, nor

What all, &c. What all, &c.

will I fear What all my foes can do - - - - - - - - - - - What all my foes can do.

What all, &c. What all, &c.

CHEERFUL.

VICTORY. C. M.

Now shall my head be lifted high, A - bove my foes a - round, And songs of joy and vic - to - ry, Within thy temple sound.

DEVIZES. C. M.

Awake my soul, a - rise my tongue, pre - pare a tune - ful voice In God the life of all my joys - - -

DEVIZES, Concluded.   **TUCKER.**   VIVACE.   **BROOMSGROVE. C. M.**   7

A - loud will I re - joice, A - loud will I re - joice.

O render thanks and bless the Lord, Invoke

N. B. The above Pia. passage to be sung as a duett.

his ho - ly name, Acquaint the nations with his deeds, His match - less deeds pro - claim, His matchless deeds pro - claim.

N. B. This tune may be sung in the key of (B) if more agreeable

CLIFFORD. C. M.   Hymn 62, 1st Book. Dr, Watts.

Come let us join our cheer - ful songs, With an - gels round the throne; Ten thousand thou - sand are their

tongues, Ten thou - sand thou - sand are their tongues, But all their joys are one, But all their joys are one.

KNARESBOROUGH. C. M.   Hymn 54. 2d. Bk. Dr. Watts.   LEACH.

My God, the spring of all my joys, The life of my de - lights, The life of my delights, The glo - ry of my brightest

glo - ry of my brightest days,   FOR.

days, - - - - - - - - - And comfort of my nights, The glory of my brightest days, And comfort of my nights.

glo - ry of my brightest days,   FOR.

10

HORSLEY. L. M.   Psalm 19th, Dr. Watts.   Js. TUCKER.

The heav'ns declare thy glo-ry Lord, In ev-ry star thy wis-dom shines, But when our eyes behold thy word We read thy

PIA. We read thy name in   FOR.

name - - - in fairer lines, We read thy name in fairer lines.

PIA. We read thy name in   FOR.

CHEERFUL.   ANTIGUA. L. M.

The King of saints how fair his face,   Adorn'd with

ma - jes - ty and grace! He comes with blessings from a - bove, And wins the na - tions by his love.

VIGOROSO.

LUTON. L. M.

Rev. G. Burder.

ALTO.

TENOR.

With all my pow'r of heart and tongue, I'll praise my Maker in my song, Angels will hear the notes I raise; Approve the song and join the praise

TREBLE.

12 VIGOROSO.   CHINA. L. M.   Hymn 127, Bk. 1st. Dr. Watts.   B Cuzens

ALTO.

TENOR.   PIA.

Come hither all ye weary souls, Ye heavy laden sinners come,   I'll give you rest from all your toils, And bring you to my heav'nly home,

TREBLE.

PIA.

CHORUS TO CHINA, or any other suitable tune.

FOR.   Come and welcome, :||:

I'll give you rest from all your toils, And bring you to my heav'n - ly home.   AFFETUOSO.   CHORUS. VIVACE.

FOR.   Come   to   Jesus,   Come and welcome, :||:

come and welcome, Come,   Come and welcome, :||:   :||:   Come, Come and welcome sinners come.

AFFETUOSO.   CHORUS VIVACE.   FORTIS.

come and welcome, Come, come to Jesus, Come and welcome, :||:   :||:   Come, come and welcome, sinners come.

TRURO. L. M.   Hymn 47, Bk. 2d. Dr. Watts.   From HANDEL

ALTO.

TENOR.

Now to the Lord a noble song, Awake my soul, awake my tongue,   Ho-sanna to th' eternal name,   And all his boundless love proclaim.

TREBLE.

CREATION. L. M.   Psalm. 117, Dr. Watts   Adapted from HAYDN.

From all that dwell be - low the skies, Let the cre - a - tor's praise a - rise, Let the Redeemer's name be sung, Through

N. B. The Pia. passage in this tune, to be performed with

ev' - ry land by ev' - ry tongue, Let the Re - deem - er's name be sung, Through ev' - ry land by ev' - ry tongue.

GRATITUDE. P. M. 8, 7, 8, 7, 4, 7. Hymn 341, Lady Huntingdon's Col. and 108, Rippon's.

MAESTOSO.

Now we'd all with grateful spirits, Join to bless the prince of peace, Praise him for imparted favors, :||:

Praise, &c.

Praise, &c.

Praise him for displays of grace, Love - ly tem - ple, Love - ly temple, Lovely temple, When the Saviour's in the place.

Love - ly tem - ple, Lovely temple, Lovely, &c.

Love - ly

ANDANTE.

NEWCOURT. L. P. M. 8, 8, 8, 8, 8, 8.

H. BOND.

Great God, the heav'ns well order'd frame, Declares the glo-ry of thy name; There thy rich works of won-der shine,

A thou-sand star-ry beau-ties there, A thousand radiant marks ap - pear, Of boundless pow'r and skill di vine.

Glory   to God on high, Let earth and skies reply, Praise ye his name,   His love and grace adore, Who all our sorrows bore, Sing aloud

ev - ermore, Worthy the Lamb,   Worthy the Lamb,   Worthy the Lamb,   Sing aloud ev - ermore, Worthy the Lamb.

18

RAPTURE. C. P. M, 8, 8, & 6. or L. P. M. 8, 8, 8, 8, 8, 8,

By omitting the slurs, and putting four syllables in the bars marked thus. (*)

HARWOOD.

CHEERFUL

ALTO.

TENOR.

PIA. 2ND. TREBLE.

Begin my soul th' ex-al-ted lay, Let each in-rap - tur'd thought obey, And praise th' Almigty's name, Let heav'n, and earth, and

TREBLE.

God is our ref - uge in distress, A present help when dangers press; In him undaunted we'll confide, Tho' earth were from her

PIA.

CRES

FOR.

TENOR.

seas and skies, In one melodious concert rise, To swell th' inspiring theme.

CRES.

FOR.

centre tost, And mountains in the ocean lost, Torn peacemeal by the roaring tide.

MAESTOSO.

HYMN FOR NEW YEAR. Eights.

ALTO.

TENOR.

Great God, we sing thy mighty hand, By which

TREBLE.

sung to any L. M. HYMN OF PSALM, by

sup - ported still we stand, The op'ning year thy mercy shows, Let mercy crown it till it close, Let mercy crown it till it close. The op'ning

year thy mercy shows, Let mercy crown it till it close, Let mercy crown it till it close, till it close, Let mercy crown it till it close.

GREENVILLE. P. M. 7s. six lines, or 8, 7, 8, 7, 4, 4, 7.

By omitting the slurs in bars marked thus, (*)

AFFETUOSO.

TENOR.

FINE.

DA CAPO.

Children of the heav'nly King, As ye journey sweet-ly sing! Sing your Saviour's worthy praise, Glorious in his works and ways;

TREBLE.

FINE.

DA CAPO.

Sing your Saviour's worthy praise, Glorious in his works and ways.

FINE.

Gently Lord, O gently lead us, Thro' this lowly vale of tears, And, O Lord, in mercy give us, Thy rich grace in all our fears!
Oh! refresh us, Oh! refresh us, Oh! refresh us with thy grace.

ANDANTE. EXPRESSIVO.   TAMWORTH. P. M. 8, 7, 4, 4, 7.   C. LOCKHEART.

ALTO.   LARGO.   TEMPO.

TENOR.   PIA.   FOR.

Guide me O thou great Je-hovah, Pilgrim thro' this barren land;
I am weak, but thou art mighty, Hold me with thy pow'rful hand; Bread of heaven, Bread of heaven, Feed me till I want no more.

TREBLE.

PIA.   FOR.

ANTHEM.

"O praise the Lord in that blest place."

C. Meinecke.

O praise the Lord in that blest place, From whence his goodness large - ly flows, Praise him in heav'n, where he his face Unveil'd in per - fect glory shows, Unveil'd in perfect glory shows

VOLTI

CHORUS. SPIRITOSO

ALTO

TENOR.

Praise him for all,   Praise him for all,   Praise him for all   the   mighty acts,   Praise him for all,   Praise him for all, Praise him for all the

TREBLE.

With which   With

mighty acts, Which he in our   behalf has done, His kindness this return exacts, With which our praise should equal run, Should equal run, With

With which

TREBLE. DIVIDED.   With
TREBLE. DIVIDED.

which our praise should e-qual run.

Let the shrill trumpet's warlike voice,

Let the shrill trumpet's warlike voice, Make rocks and hills his praise rebound,

Let the shrill trumpet's

warlike voice, Make rocks and hills his praise rebound, Make ro-cks and hills his praise rebound.

FIRST TREBLE. VERSE GRAZIOSO.

Praise him with harp's me - lodious noise, And gen - tle psaltry's sil - ver sound; Praise him with harp's me - lo - dious noise, And gen - tle

SECOND TREBLE.

SYM. ALLEGRETTO.

psal - try's sil - ver sound.

Let virgin troops soft timbrels

bring, And some with grace - ful mo - tion dance, Let vir - gin troops soft tim - brels bring, And some with grace - ful mo - tion dance.

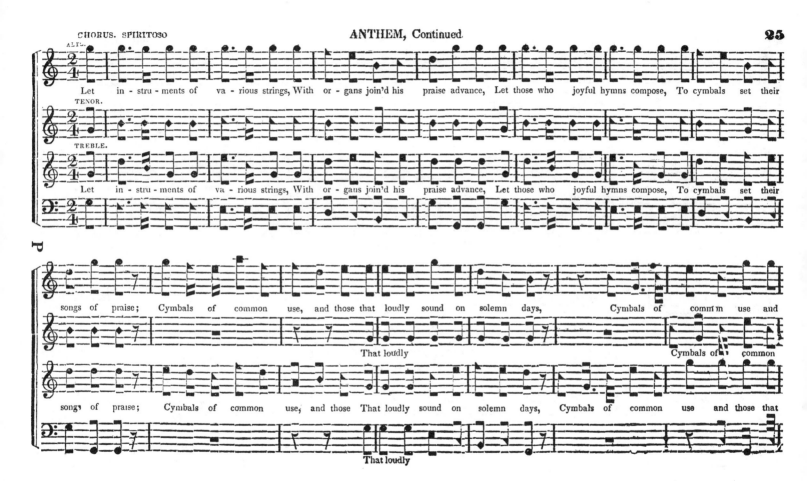

CHORUS. SPIRITOSO

ALTO.

Let in - stru - ments of va - rious strings, With or - gans join'd his praise advance, Let those who joyful hymns compose, To cymbals set their

TENOR.

TREBLE.

Let in - stru - ments of va - rious strings, With or - gans join'd his praise advance, Let those who joyful hymns compose, To cymbals set their

P

songs of praise; Cymbals of common use, and those that loudly sound on solemn days, Cymbals of common use and

That loudly

Cymbals of common

songs of praise; Cymbals of common use, and those That loudly sound on solemn days, Cymbals of common use and those that

That loudly

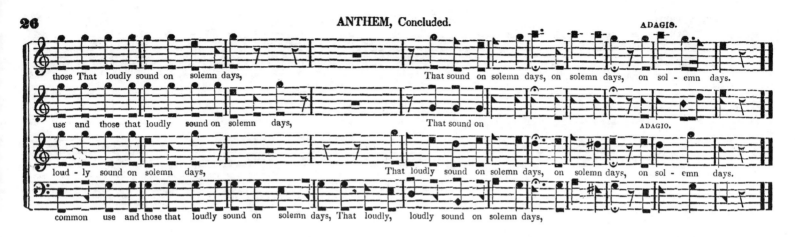

those That loudly sound on solemn days, That sound on solemn days, on solemn days, on sol-emn days.

use and those that loudly sound on solemn days, That sound on

loud-ly sound on solemn days, That loudly sound on solemn days, on solemn days, on sol-emn days.

common use and those that loudly sound on solemn days, That loudly, loudly sound on solemn days,

FULL CHORUS. MAESTOSO.

Let all who vital breath enjoy, The breath he doth to them af-ford, In just returns of praise employ, Let ev'ry creature praise the Lord, Amen, Amen.

VIGOROSO.

ALTO.

TENOR.

Beyond, Beyond the glitt'ring starry skies, Far as th' eter - nal hills, Far as th' e - ternal hills; There in the boundless realms of light Our

TREBLE.

DUETTO. TREBLE AND BASS.

GRAZIOSO. Im - mor - tal Angels bright and fair, In countless ar - mies shine, At

dear Re - deem - er dwells, Our dear Redeem - er dwells.

his right hand with gol - den harps they of - fer songs di - vine, At his right

FULL CHORUS. SPIRITOSO.

hand with gol - den harps, They

of - fer songs di - vine.

ALTO.

TENOR.

TREBLE. They brought his Chariot from above, To bear him to his throne; Clapp'd their tri-

umphant, Clapp'd their tri - umphant wings and cry'd, The glo - rious work is done.

The foregoing piece is also well adapted to the following words, from Hymn 1st. Book 1st. Dr. Watts.

Behold, :‖: the glories of the Lamb,
    Amidst his Father's throne; :‖:
Prepare new honors for his name,
    And songs before unknown. :‖:

DUETTO.
Let Elders worship at his feet,
    The church adore around;
With vials full of odors sweet,
    And harps of sweeter sound.
                    With vials full, &c

CHORUS.
Now to the Lamb that once was slain
    Be endless blessings paid;
Salvation, glory, :‖: joy remain,
    Forever on his head.

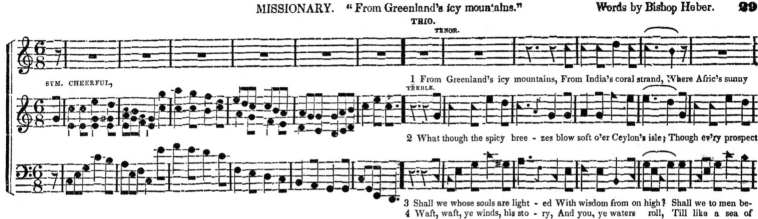

TRIO.
TENOR.
SYM. CHEERFUL,
TREBLE.

1 From Greenland's icy mountains, From India's coral strand, Where Afric's sunny

2 What though the spicy bree - zes blow soft o'er Ceylon's isle; Though ev'ry prospect

3 Shall we whose souls are light - ed With wisdom from on high? Shall we to men be-
4 Waft, waft, ye winds, his sto - ry, And you, ye waters roll, Till like a sea of

PIA.
FOR.
fountains, Roll down their golden sand, From many an ancient river,
From many a palmy plain, They call us to de - liv - er Their land from error's chain,

PIA.
FOR.
pleases, And on - ly man is vile: In vain with lavish kindness,
The gifts of God are strown; The heathen in his blindness, Bows down to wood and stone.

nighted, The lamp of life de - ny? Salva - tion! Oh Salva - tion!
The joyful sound pre - claim, Till earth's re - mo - test na - tion, Has learn'd Messiah's name.

glo - ry, It spreads from pole to pole; Till o'er our ransom'd nature,
The Lamb for sinners slain, Redeem - er, King, Cre - a - tor, Returns in bliss to reign.
VOLTI CHORUS.

FULL CHORUS. VIGOROSO.   MISSIONARY, Concluded.

Sal - va - tion! Oh, sal - va - tion! The joy - ful sound pro - claim; Till earth's re - mo - test

na - tion, Has learn'd Mes - si - ah's name; Till earth's re - mo - test na - tion, Has learn'd Mes - si - ah's name,

ALL THINGS FAIR AND BRIGHT ARE THINE.

A DUETT, BY O. SHAW.

ARRANGED FOR THE ORGAN OR PIANO FORTE.

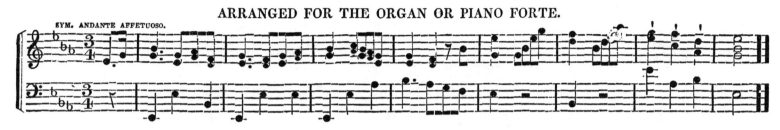

Thou art, O God, the life and light, Of all this wond-rous world we see. Its glow by

VOLTI SUBITO

DUETT, Continued.

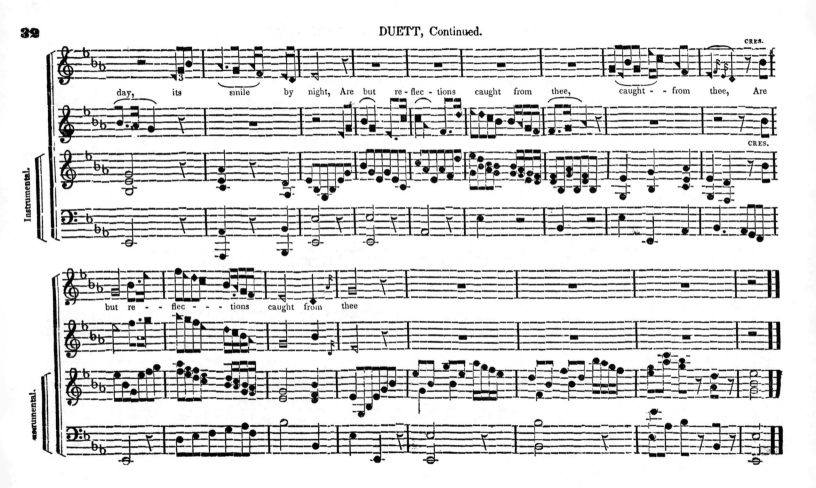

day, its smile by night, Are but re - flec - tions caught from thee, caught - from thee, Are

Instrumental.

but re - flec - - tions caught from thee

Instrumental.

Where'er we turn, thy glo - ries shine, And all things fair and bright are thine.   Where'er we

turn, Where'er we turn, thy glo-ries shine,   And all   things fair   and bright are thine,

Instrumental.

DUETT, Concluded.

And all things fair — — — and bright are thine, — are thine, And all things fair — — — and

bright are thine.

2nd. Verse.

When youthful spring around us breathes,
Thy spirit warms her fragrant sigh;
And every flower the summer wreathes,
Is borne beneath that kindling eye.
Where'er we turn, thy glories shine,
And all things fair and bright are thine.

A SACRED SONG BY O. SHAW, ARRANGED FOR THE ORGAN OR PIANO FORTE.

This world is all a fleet-ing show, for man's illu-sion giv'n, This world is all a fleet-ing show for man's il-lu-sion giv

36

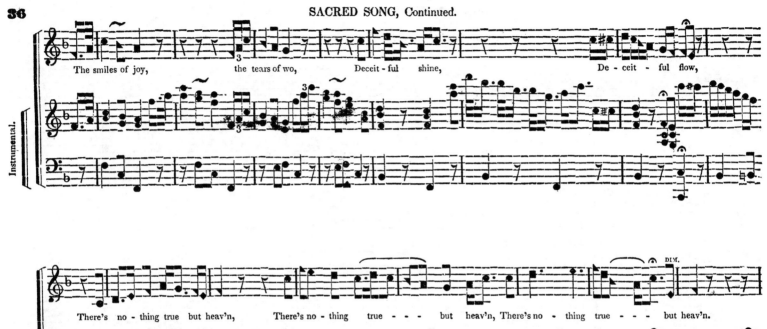

2d. Verse.

And false the light on glory's plume, as fading hues of even;
  And love, and hope, and beauty's bloom
Are blossoms gather'd for the tomb—
  There's nothing bright but heav'n!

3d. Verse.

Poor wand'rers of a stormy day, from wave to wave we're driv'n,
  And fancy's flash and reason's ray,
Serve but to light the troubled wav—
  There's nothing calm but heav'n!

N. B. In singing the third line of the 2nd. verse, after applying the words " Are blossoms gather'd" to the 4th and 5th bars, from the double bar, untie the six semiquavers in the 7th bar and apply the whole of said third line to the 6th and 7th bars: And in singing the third line of the third verse, after applying the words " Serve but to light" to the 4th and 5th bars, apply the whole of said line to the 6th and 7th bars, in the same manner as directed for the third line of the 2nd verse

BLESSED BE THE LORD FOREVERMORE.

Rev. A. Thompson.

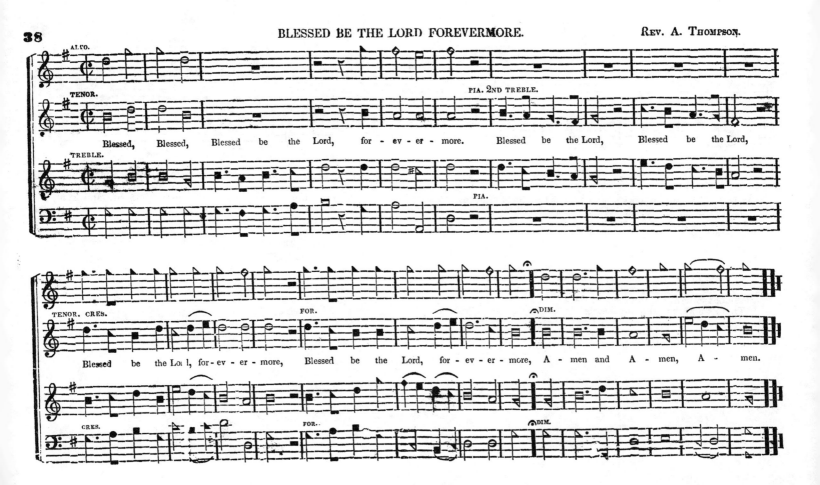

Blessed, Blessed, Blessed be the Lord, for - ev - er - more. Blessed be the Lord, Blessed be the Lord,

Blessed be the Lord, for - ev - er - more, Blessed be the Lord, for - ev - er - more, A - men and A - men, A - men.

GENERAL INDEX OF TUNES, &c., CONTAINED IN THE FORMER PART OF THIS WORK.

INDEX TO THE SUPPLEMENT.